REFLECTIONS OF GOD

REFLECTIONS OF GOD

David Delich, O.P.

A SHEED & WARD BOOK

ROWMAN & LITTLEFIELD PUBLISHERS, INC.
Lanham • Boulder • New York • Toronto • Plymouth, UK

A SHEED & WARD BOOK

ROWMAN & LITTLEFIELD PUBLISHERS, INC.
Published in the United States of America
by Rowman & Littlefield Publishers, Inc.
A wholly owned subsidary of The Rowman & Littlefield Publishing Group, Inc.
4501 Forbes Boulevard, Suite 200, Lanham, Maryland 20706
www.rowmanlittlefield.com

Estover Road, Plymouth PL6 7PY, United Kingdom

Printed in the United States of America

Cover and interior photography by David Delich, O.P.

Cover and Interior Design by GrafixStudio, Inc.

Chapter 2 and Chapter 3 have been previously published in *U.S. Catholic*
(Chicago, Illinois.)

Library of Congress Cataloging-in--Publication Data

Delich, Dave.
        Reflections of God / by Dave Delich.
                p. cm.
        ISBN 1-58051-066-3 (alk. paper)
                1. God Meditations. 2. Spiritual life—Catholic Church Meditations.
        I. Title.
        BT102 .D45 1999
242—dc21
                                                                        99-16892
                                                                        CIP

Contents

Preface

This book is a collection of biblical analogies. My purpose is to make God, the Unknowable, a little less unknowable. Some of the figures are from the Bible itself and others are my own creation. Jesus, the master teacher and preacher, used many metaphors, figures, and parables in his preaching and teaching. His use of them though, is perplexing to say the least. Two quotations from Mark 4 will highlight the problem: "Now when he was away from the crowd, those present with the Twelve questioned him about the parables. He told them: 'To you the mystery of the reign of God has been confided. To the others outside it is all presented in parables, so that they will look intently and not see, listen carefully and not understand, lest perhaps they repent and be forgiven'" (Mk 4:10–12). "He went on to say: 'What comparison shall we use for the reign of

God? What image will help to present it? It is like mustard seed . . .'" (Mk 4:30–31). The first passage makes the point that Jesus used parables to teach the crowds in a rudimentary and incomplete manner—only later would he further explain the parable to his inner circle of disciples. The implication here is that he taught the crowds to the extent that they were able to understand and accept new ideas. The second quotation is much more positive with regard to the use of figures. Here Jesus seems to use parables and figures to better get across an idea. These two quotations are apparently contradictory—the real truth of the matter will probably remain forever elusive. Never having been much inclined to the *Via Negativa*, I tend to go with the latter interpretation. I'm definitely of the school that holds that a picture, even a mental picture, is worth a thousand words. My bias stems from teaching physics, that most abstruse of subjects, to high school students. Therefore my purpose in this book is to supply pictures, hopefully unforgettable pictures, that will lead to a deeper knowledge of God. Also it is my hope that the pictures in this book will stimulate you to search for your own pictures in your picture albums.

Before you begin reading I have, at the risk of embarrassment, a confession to make. After writing this book I sat and asked myself which of these pictures of God I liked most. My first choice was easy: Jesus, *the* icon of God (see Chapter 21). My second choice took longer to arrive at and when it came, I couldn't believe it. In fact, I still can't believe it because it's me (see Chapter 4). . . . I'm blushing.

David Delich, O.P.
10/11/99

1
God Makes All Things Work Together for the Good of Those Who Love Him

We know that God makes all things work together for the good of those who have been called according to his decree. . . . Who will separate us from the love of Christ? Trial, or distress, or persecution, or hunger, or nakedness, or danger, or the sword? . . . I am certain that neither death, nor life, neither angels nor principalities, neither the present nor the future, nor powers, neither height nor depth nor any other creature, will be able to separate us from the love of God that comes to us in Christ Jesus, our Lord. (Rom 8:28, 35, 38–39)

Of all the problems of human existence, evil is the greatest. How does one reconcile an all-knowing, all-loving, and all-powerful God with the evil which touches us almost every day, either personally or vicariously in the pain and suffering of others? This is no easy task. Many give up. They either fall into disbelief or change their concept of God. Rabbi Kuschner, the author of the best-seller, *When Bad Things Happen to Good People*, chooses to believe that God is all-loving, but not all-powerful—if he were, he would put an end to evil and the human suffering that follows in its wake.

Several years back I was on a plane reading the airline's periodical. My attention was drawn to the picture of a Dominican friar dressed in full white habit (try to reconcile that with the fact that we have the nickname *Blackfriars*). It turned out that the article was about a famous geneticist at a California university (his name eludes me) who used to be a Dominican. He lost his faith over the problem of evil. How could a loving all-powerful God exist when so many babies are born with serious birth defects? My own view of evil is more restrained, and perhaps influenced by my background in physics. Given a universe governed by ineluctable physical laws such as those of gravity and magnetism, there is going to be evil. People will fall from windows. People will be struck by lightening. And so on. You can't have it both ways; either the world will be governed by physical laws or God will have to control all events on a one-to-one basis. What amazes me is the interconnectedness of the universe—so many laws and so many agents all coming together to produce such marvelous results. Given the complexity of gestation, the real miracle is that any child is born without defect. Of course, it's easy to pontificate on birth defects if one doesn't have children with birth defects—there's that old proverb: "It depends on whose ox is being gored." It's one thing to reconcile evil which comes about by the interplay of physical laws, and quite another to reconcile evil which is malevolent—and the twentieth century has had more of that than any previous century, arguably more than that of all previous centuries put together.

The Bible is remarkably silent on the problem of evil. The prevailing view of the Old Testament is that those who suffer, suffer because of their sins—the Book of Job corrects that view. Jesus also attempts to correct that theology in Luke 13: "Do you think that these Galileans were the greatest sinners in Galilee just because they suffered this? By no means!" St. Paul, in Romans 5, teaches that death and other forms of evil entered the world in the wake of Adam's sin. The most explicit biblical teaching about sin is Romans 8:28: "We know that God makes all things work together for the good of those who have been called according to his decree. . . ." "All things" includes evil. In other words, God is able to write straight with crooked lines. All this boils down to "Keep walking, and believe in God's love. His love is there, even in the midst of the evil you are suffering. Have faith." This is precious little explanation. The problem with "makes all things work together" is that sometimes we don't see that they work together until after we die. This was the case in the greatest illustration of Romans 8:28, namely, the crucifixion, death, and resurrection of Jesus. Here in these events we have the one most loved by God suffering the most of all. Seemingly abandoned by God, Jesus dies, but God raises him up and makes him Lord of all creation. Since, the "work together" is not always perceived, we have to simply believe. In many instances evil remains a mystery.

In a lighter vein, I can illustrate Romans 8:28 with a chapter from my own life. When I was a young Dominican studying philosophy, I began to be troubled by failing eyesight in my left eye. We used to spend our summers up at our camp north of Menomonee, Michigan. I went to have this checked out by the eye doctor in Menomonee. He had me read the seventh line of the chart with my left eye. I was unable to read it and told him so. His response was, "If you really wanted to you could." I was so taken back by those words that I have no recollection of what happened after that. I left the office feeling like a hopeless hypochondriac. In the ensuing years my vision got even worse, but I was afraid to go to the doctor. I certainly wouldn't have gone back to that doctor, but I was afraid to go to any doctor—one can take only so much abuse! (I seem to be in an anti-doctor mood today. If you are a doctor, substitute the word "priest" for "doctor," if needs be.)

Finally, many years later, I did go back to see an eye doctor. He examined my left eye and was appalled by what he saw. "What happened to your left eye?," he asked. "It looks like someone hit you with a baseball bat; I don't think much can be done for it." Shortly after that I suffered a retinal detachment in my left eye. I say "suffered" because I had three cryo-therapies on the eye—emphasis on "cry," and more than enough pain for a lifetime! The therapy was inefficacious and I became totally blind in my left eye within a month. The miracle is that I see better now than before I went blind!

I forgot to mention that two years before I went to that mean old doctor in Menomonee, I developed *hypertropia*, commonly called "double vision." I used to say that double vision is great if you're with friends. So you see, I do see better now than before I went blind. Blindness cured my double vision—now I don't see double!

My story is somewhat facetious because of my double vision twist. Normally, losing sight in one eye is a bigger loss than the loss I experienced. I notice that insurance policies give half of a death benefit for accidents that cause blindness in one eye. I always say that if I ever become blind in the other eye I won't be so glib about it. However, just today I talked to a totally blind lady to whom I was apologizing. She had come up to me at mass for communion. I gave her husband communion but passed her up—she was on my blind side. Luckily she didn't see the oversight! I asked her about Romans 8:28 relative to her total blindness. She said that Romans 8:28 was true in her case, that blindness protected her against seeing a lot that others wish they hadn't seen. She wasn't quite so sure about whether her husband could say the same; she feared that her blindness put a lot of burdens on him.

I'll end this chapter with a vignette about something that I've experienced over and over again. I must preface it with the fact that over the years my blind eye has drifted to the left—to the extent that I can't ask questions of an audience when I'm giving a sermon. If I do ask a question and recognize a raised hand, about twenty people start speaking. I was a full time hospital chaplain for a ten-year period which ended in 1996. Many times I would be alone with a patient in a private room administering communion. When I would hold up the host and say, "the body of Christ," the patient would reply, "Do you mean me?" At that point I would have to leave the room for a good laugh.

Suffering and evil remain the greatest of human mysteries. This is an area of life wherein we need faith in a loving God. Chapter 21 of this book will look at Jesus as "icon of God." In the eyes of the crucified Jesus, we will see the eyes of a loving Father. This vision will sustain us as we face the evil that is certain to come our way.

2

See, I Am Doing
Something New

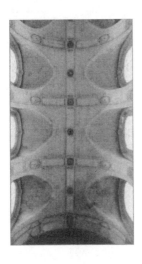

Remember not the events of the past,
the things of long ago consider not;
See, I am doing something new!
Now it springs forth,
do you not perceive it? . . .
For I put water in the desert
and rivers in the wasteland
for my chosen people to drink,
The people whom I formed for myself,
that they might announce my praise.
(Is 43:18–21)

I now read the messianic prophecies differently—without the disappointment I previously experienced because of the glacially slow growth, if any, of the kingdom of God over the past twenty centuries since Christ inaugurated the messianic kingdom of God. The reason for my newfound comfort is that I no longer read the prophecies of Isaiah as literally as I used to. This was my mistake and the mistake, I believe, of the Church in general with regard to these messianic texts. I don't mean to be overly critical, since an overly literal interpretation is an inherent temptation built into the texts themselves. During Advent the Church reads Isaiah's messianic prophecies at mass and then reads a gospel passage which fulfills the prophecy. The fulfillment texts generally stick pretty close to a literal reading of the prophetic texts. For example: "And out of gloom and darkness,/the eyes of the blind shall see" (Is 29:18). And

"'Because of your faith it shall be done to you;' and they recovered their sight" (Mt 9:29–30). I find no problem with the healing passages—it's a gospel assertion that Jesus healed physical disease in his ministry. However, I used to have a problem with regard to the continuation of Jesus' healing in the present day. (One of the assumptions of a literal interpretation of Isaiah is that the kingdom to be inaugurated by the Messiah is ever growing into something more perfect). At times I bought into various aspects of that premise, not however with regard to my own physical healing—having been half blind for twenty-five years, I long ago gave up on seeing again with my left eye this side of the Second Coming of Christ, the messianic kingdom notwithstanding. The gospel passages somewhat dull the edge of a literalist interpretation of the healing passages of Isaiah in that healing of the deaf and the blind is inclusive of a spiritual meaning of blindness and deafness—and of course, present-day grace is able to heal spiritually.

Isaiah's passages pointing to the coming messianic kingdom describe a kingdom in which want and need are replaced with plenty, ignorance with knowledge, sickness with healing and, finally, injustice, oppression, and violence with peace, justice, and well-being. My Achilles tendon in reading these passages literally came from what I now consider an unwarranted expectation of peace and justice. Consider these texts: "They shall beat their swords into plowshares. . . . /One nation shall not raise the sword against another, / nor shall they train for war again" (Is 2:4). "The tyrant will be no more / and the arrogant will have gone" (Is 29: 20).

The alleviation of violence is not one of the strong hallmarks of our century. In fact, without doubt, the twentieth century has been more violent than any which preceded it. There are plenty of Hitler-like despots to be found. And what is even more disconcerting is the degree of institutional and nationalistic violence. Recently I read that on one night during May of 1945 over three hundred thousand Japanese civilians were killed in Tokyo by incendiary bombs—and violence and killing has not abated over the past fifty years.

Sadly, I don't experience the world, let alone the kingdom of God, getting better and better. As far as I can see, the world has made precious little progress since Jesus inaugurated the kingdom twenty centuries ago. My life experience is mixed. Some things are better now than when I came into the world, and some things are a lot worse—not that there is a causal connection between the latter and my birth. Perhaps I'm becoming cynical as I get older—certainly a recent trip to Guatemala and El Salvador didn't improve a somewhat pessimistic life view. My read on civilization's progress is that it is not at all like a graph of the Dow Jones over the past fifty years, i.e., a relatively straight line with a positive slope. It's more like one day of the Dow, a graph characterized by a lot of ups and downs.

What can be said about a kingdom of ever increasing peace and justice. Our faith tells us that eventually peace and justice will be constitutive parts of the kingdom. The real question is, "When?" Are we making any progress on the path to greater peace and justice? Or will it come all at once as part of the parousia? The question at hand is whether Isaiah prophesied ever increasing peace and justice as components of the messianic kingdom in all stages of its development. I answer in the negative. A closer examination of the texts shows that the nonviolence parts of the texts are not to be taken literally but are to be taken as indicative of the startling and unusual ways in which God is going to break in as he establishes the messianic kingdom. This, to my mind, is what Isaiah is primarily saying in these texts. When God breaks into our human condition, he's going to do it in unexpected, remarkable, and unique ways. "Remember not the events of the past, / the things of long ago consider not; / See, I am doing something new! / Now it springs forth, do you not perceive it?" (Is 43:18–19) "One nation shall not raise the sword against another." How's that for something remarkable and unusual! This sentence is, however, not a prophecy but simply an example of the unexpected and remarkable. Notice how all the other previously cited verses and the following verses of Isaiah fall into place if we interpret them not as literal prophecy but as examples of the unexpected and unusual ways of God:

"The calf and the young lion shall browse together" (Is 11:6). And, "But a very little while, / and Lebanon shall be changed into an orchard" (Is 29:17). The image of Lebanon, noted for its cedar forests, turned into an orchard presents an unforgettable picture of the unexpected and the unusual.

Acts provides an interesting illustration of this thesis. In the most passionate preaching of their first missionary journey, Paul and Barnabas boldly preach that the cross of Jesus brings acquittal for sins. They then warn their audience not to fulfill the Isaian-like prophecy of Habakkuk 1:5 by their unbelief: "'Look on, you scoffers, / be amazed and disappear. / For I am doing a work in your days, / a work that you will never believe even if someone / tells you'" (Acts 13:41).

If this is the primary purpose of Isaiah's texts, that is, to get across the point that God is about to do something unique, we don't have to look very far to see that this is exactly what God has done in the life, words, and message of Jesus. The primary startling uniqueness of the gospel is its universalism—everyone falls in the ambit of God's love and forgiveness. Even the non-Jew is loved by God! Even the most undeserving is forgiven by God! Nothing like this had ever been heard before. Another significant unique facet of the gospel, of the startling reversal of position: the last shall be first and, in some sense, the first shall be last. After two thousand years the Church is still trying to wrap its mind and behavior around this last point, even though Jesus gave us an adequate example of his words: "The first among you shall be the last and the servant of all."

I have a life experience metaphor that images God's startling and unexpected ways: the universal forgiveness of the cross—this figure is one of my favorites. Twenty-five years ago my religious community moved lock, stock, and cats to a turn-of-the-century house in Oak Park, Illinois. At the time we had two cats, a black one without papers and a young seal point Siamese, who didn't have papers but looked like he simply misplaced them. On the day of the move, one of the first things I did was to establish a cat-door. I removed one of the basement windowpanes and replaced it with a piece of plywood. I cleverly made two holes in the plywood: a rectangular hole for the cat-door apparatus and a circular hole for the dryer exhaust hose. Within a few days our cats were able to negotiate the cat-door at breakneck speeds even in the dark. In their inimitable way they could jump from the cat-door onto the washer and onto the floor in no time flat.

Several months after the move, however, my relationship with the black cat started to deteriorate. He sensed that my affections were turning to the better-looking and younger Yanko. It was a classic case of alienating affections. He jealously got back at me by getting into the garbage and dragging it from the kitchen onto what was previously our new beige dining room rug. This sinful behavior cried out for requital. After discovering one of these indiscretions I would go into a rage and search out the black cat. No matter how late it was, I would find him, pick him up, and toss him out the front door. Then, my real work began: I had to run down the basement stairs as fast as I could, take the twenty-pound box of Tide sitting alongside the washer and slam it in front of the cat-door. I wanted that cat out of my life forever! In this little story, I play the role of God. You can see how little I resemble God in the end—if you had any doubts about the matter in the beginning. The cross of Jesus and its fruit, universal forgiveness, is the cat-door. It provides free access into the house (read kingdom) at all times—even for undeserving cats. However, God, unlike me, never repents about establishing the cat-door in the first place.

"As high as the heavens are above the earth, / so high are my ways above your ways" (Is 55:9). Has anyone ever seen the likes of such generosity and love, such compassion and forgiveness? This is the new and unexpected to which the messianic passages of Isaiah point. "See, I am doing something new!" Once we see it, we cannot but be a people that announces God's praise.

3

Jesus' Selfish Love

Praised be the God and Father of our Lord Jesus Christ, who has bestowed on us in Christ every spiritual blessing in the heavens! God chose us in him . . . to be holy and blameless in his sight, to be full of love; he likewise predestined us through Christ Jesus to be his adopted sons. . . . Both with and in Christ Jesus he raised us up and gave us a place in the heavens, that in the ages to come he might display the great wealth of his favor, manifested by his kindness to us in Christ Jesus. . . . We are truly his handiwork.(Eph 1:3–2:10)

What wealth of revelation is contained in this passage of holy Scripture. The magnitude and excellence of what God has given us in Christ is breathtaking. God has already raised us up with Christ Jesus and has placed us with him at his right hand (Eph 1:20). Even now he is displaying us in the heavens as his handiwork. Once, while preaching on this text to school children, I asked if anyone knew what "handiwork" was. One girl thought it meant taking out the garbage. After I got her on track she said that handiwork was like a sweater she had just knitted and of which she was very proud. She was thrilled to think of herself as one of God's sweaters—this revelation makes us far greater than one of God's sweaters.

The many references to Christ in the above text imply that the grace given is not just a gift but a gift relating us to

Christ and conforming us to the image of Christ. It's common now to retranslate adopted "sons" to "sons and daughters" or "children." The recent *New American Bible* translates the phrase as "he destined us for adoption to himself through Jesus Christ." My preference is to leave it as "sons" because the phrase has a reference not to "son" but to "Son." Paul is trying to tell us that grace makes us into an adopted Jesus. "Adopted" here does not have a pejorative connotation; Paul simply wants to differentiate our sonship from that of Jesus, in that ours came about in time, not from all eternity. In other words, through grace we become in God's eyes his beloved, his Jesus! When we pray we can address God as "Abba," a term that only Jesus could use (Mk 14:36, Rom 8:15). When we pray we can even dare to say to God, "Look at me, Abba, I am your Jesus."

Galatians 3 and 4 provides much additional light on sanctifying grace and its product: *divinization in Christ:* "Each one of you is a son of God, because of your faith in Christ Jesus. All of you who have been baptized into Christ have clothed yourselves with him. There does not exist among you Jew or Greek, slave or freeman, male or female. All are one in Christ Jesus." Here again I prefer to leave the translation as "son" rather than "child" or "son or daughter" because the reference is again to Son, i.e., Jesus. The figure of clothing is very apt here in leading us into a deeper understanding of the truth about sanctifying grace. A truth that is startling: "You . . . have clothed yourselves with him," meaning you have put on Christ, you have become Christ. In other passages where Paul uses the clothing figure, the meaning is that we must put on the virtues of Christ (Col 3:10–12). In Galatians 3 the meaning is more in the essential order and much deeper. The real proof of this is in "There does not exist . . . male or female. All are one in Christ Jesus." Today this text is frequently used to teach that essential equality exists in the Church between men and women. However true that thesis might be, I don't think that Paul is teaching that truth in this passage. If that's what he meant, he would have written: "All are one." "All are one in Christ Jesus" means something else. "All are one" would mean that no distinction can be made between members of the body. "All are one in Christ Jesus" means that no distinction can be made between members of the body and Christ Jesus! What a comforting thought when we ponder our relationship with God, especially at times when he seems distant. He cannot but love us because as long as we are in Christ Jesus no distinction can be made between him and us! This is not to say that grace makes us divine. Rather, it makes us beautiful, good, and lovable in God's eyes. Just as Jesus, through grace, was made God's beloved, so does that same grace make us God's beloved. This is revelation of the highest order.

Recently, while I was giving a homily on these clothing texts at the federal penitentiary in Chicago's Loop, I came close to experiencing their full meaning. I suddenly realized that all the prisoners bore a striking similarity to one another in that all of them were wearing orange jumpsuits. Some time in the late 1970s I experienced something similar. The incident has a *Grand Guignol* quality about it, but it is worth mentioning because it will leave a lasting memory and will prepare for my unfulfilled fantasy concerning the clothing texts. A group of my "friends" paid me a visit on Halloween. As soon as I opened the door for them at about midnight, they forced their way into the front room of the priory. It was horrible! Each was wearing a Richard Nixon mask. Mutely, they stared at me for several minutes and then left. To this day I don't know who they were. It was like being surrounded by aliens—I actually feared abduction.

My positive fantasy, which will not likely be fulfilled unless I am elected pope, consists in celebrating mass with a large congregation on Easter morning. As each worshiper enters the church, he or she will be vested with a Jesus costume complete with a Jesus mask. I realize that a lot of expense and time will be required for this liturgical *tour de force*, but it will be well worth it. Imagine attending Easter mass surrounded by this "body of Christ"—a truly unforgettable experience.

Our unity with Christ and one another is also taught by Paul using the figure of the body. To my mind the body figure is the greatest of all the analogies used in the Bible.

While the figure is used by Paul several times, for our purposes Ephesians 5:22–30 is the best reference: "Wives should be submissive to their husbands as if to the Lord. . . . Husbands, love your wives, as Christ loved the church. . . . Husbands should love their wives as they do their own bodies. He who loves his wife loves himself. Observe that no one ever hates his own flesh; he nourishes it and takes care of it as Christ cares for the church—for we are members of his body." This text also contains high revelation, but it presently suffers low esteem because of the first sentence. The true meaning of "Wives should be submissive to their husbands" is extremely moot and controversial today. Are we to understand these words literally and in a normative way, or is Paul simply reflecting the mentality and culture of his time and place? I think that the Promise Keepers brought on themselves much of their bad press before their 1997 meeting in Washington because of their statements concerning Ephesians 5:22. They would have had more than enough agenda to keep busy without touching Ephesians 5:22. Submission, however, whether normative or culturally determined, is not the major point of the text in question. The major point here is that Christ's love for us is a selfish love in that he loves us as self. He loves the Church as self! He loves me as self! How is that for good news, good news too good to be true! In other words, just as God doesn't differentiate between us and Jesus, Jesus doesn't differentiate between us and himself because we are his body. As long as we are in Christ he cannot but love us because he loves himself. This is the heart of the doctrine of the Mystical Body of Christ—an unfortunate use of the word "mystical" because, as Paul describes this reality, it is more real than real.

While the above text is explicitly directed to spouses, it is implicitly directed to all members of the Church. I can add a personal illustration of the body analogy. Six years ago I suffered one of the worst one hundred traumas of my life. I was "chef of the day," preparing a Christmas dinner of wild geese for some visiting friars from other houses as well as members of the Dominican priory in Madison, Wisconsin. Just before dinner, as I was sharpening the carving knife, disaster struck. The knife skipped out of the V-shaped Chicago Cutlery sharpening rods and cut across my right hand. The device was without the usual instruction notes, as I had bought it at a garage sale—only at that moment did it dawn on me that the unused wooden dowel was for protection of the holding hand. I knew immediately that I was in trouble because there was a lot of blood, and two of my fingers were dangling and totally unresponsive to my will. I called via the phone intercom to the recreation room where everyone was having hors d'oeuvres and told the revelers that I could use some help in the kitchen. You can imagine the ensuing scenario when two brothers arrived at the horrific scene—but enough about me. My left hand immediately and lovingly offered to help the bleeding right hand. Help was promptly accepted. Then the left hand, full of tender compassion, tightly wrapped a dish towel around the right hand to prevent further bleeding—I honestly think that the right hand would have died on the way to the hospital if the left hand had been unwilling to help. Of course, a callous response such as, "What, you need help again? I helped you last week," was out of the question because self-love was operative— the left hand perceived the right hand as self! They say every analogy eventually limps—certainly this one does when one considers who committed the crime. I was impressed with the right hand's immediate acceptance of the offer of help—perhaps it understood that the injury was unintentional—as are a good number of self-inflicted wounds in the Body of Christ. Ephesians 5 provides us with help as we try, day by day, to imitate the love and compassion of Christ. If only we could perceive others as Christ perceives us, as he perceives our bothers and sisters—as self.

Mother Teresa was often quoted as having said that if it were not for the fact that she saw Christ in those to whom she ministered, she would be incapable of serving them. I think she was really expressing the ideas from Ephesians 5. Sometimes the image of Christ is visible in the faces of our brothers and sisters. I saw him recently in the faces of the poor of Central America—though they were physically needy, their faces shone with the Lord's glory. Sometimes, however, the image of Christ in others lies hidden from our eyes. It is then that we need to invoke the power of these revelatory texts. It is then that we need to call upon our faith that all who are in Christ Jesus share in his splendor and glory, whether visible or not. St. Catherine of Siena describes in her *Dialogues* a vision she had of the beauty of someone with the least degree of sanctifying grace. The beauty was overwhelming—she confessed that she was tempted to bow down and adore the dazzlingly beautiful creature. If only we could see more of the beauty hidden within our sisters and brothers—our Church and our world would be far different than they are now. When Mother Teresa said that she saw Christ in those she served, I'm sure that sometimes she experienced St. Catherine's spirit-gift of love. Sometimes, when Christ was not so visible in her sisters and brothers, she most likely saw them with the eyes of Christ. The bottom line is that we, like Mother Teresa, are called to love our sisters and brothers. Armed with the example of Mother Teresa and these Pauline texts, may God give us the eyes of Catherine or the eyes of Jesus.

4

He Will Sing Joyfully Because of You, as One Sings at Festivals

Shout for joy, O daughter Zion!
  sing joyfully, O Israel!
Be glad and exult with all your heart,
  O daughter Jerusalem!
The LORD *has removed the*
    judgment against you.
  he has turned away your enemies....
The LORD*, your God, is in your midst,*
  a mighty savior;
He will rejoice over you with gladness,
  and renew you in his love,
He will sing joyfully because of you,
  as one sings at festivals.
(Zeph 3:14–15, 17–18)

These delightful words are read at mass on the third Sunday of Advent. They are among the most beautiful and challenging in Scripture and would be more than appropriate on any Sunday of the year since they bring out the gospel's most salient points: God's forgiveness and love. I especially like the anthropomorphism of the figure—God dancing and singing over Israel. While the words are said directly to Israel, they could just as well have been said to us. Jesus, especially in the Gospel of John, reveals that we are individually loved by God: "I have given them the glory you gave me . . . / [that] the world [may] know that you sent me, / and that you loved them as you loved me" (Jn 17:22–23). Jesus uses "as" to indicate likeness in degree. God not only loves us individually, but his love for us is similar to the love he has for Jesus. Good news too good to be true! We can all imagine God getting up and doing a jig if Jesus were to enter the room—but doing one for us? You've got to be kidding. Our faith tells us that grace conforms us to the image of Christ. St. Paul says: "All of you who have been baptized into Christ have clothed yourselves with him. There does not exist among you Jew or Greek, slave or freeman, male or female. All are one in Christ Jesus" (Gal 3:27–8). This last sentence means that grace makes us indistinguishable, not so much from one another as from Jesus himself. The figure of God, then, dancing over us, is anything but a far-fetched idea. Nonetheless, we need God's grace to grasp and accept this revelation. When was the last time you felt like singing when someone entered the room? I used to do it on a regular basis when Yanko was alive. More about him later.

There are many reasons why we have a hard time believing that God loves us. The main reason, it seems to me, is the enormous gap in "being" between him and us. How is it possible for someone so perfect, so mighty, and so wise to love little old me? Perhaps God could love me out of pity or compassion—but certainly not to the extent of dancing out of sheer delight when I enter the room. Another barrier to believing in God's love for us is the universal quality of that love. He loves each of us at all times. Whereas we love only a few people, and some of these for only a short while—until they sin against us. God loves each of us all the time, whether we're good or bad. How is it possible for God to love us when we're bad? Sometimes we're so sinful in our own eyes that even we can't love ourselves, let alone God (Eph 5:29, notwithstanding: "no one ever hates his own flesh").

This brings me back to Yanko, God's great revelatory gift to me. Yanko was a beautiful seal point Siamese. His mother, Ming-a-Ling, was my mother's pet—I called her Ding-a-Ling to my mother's everlasting annoyance. Yanko was 100% point, a remarkable fact in that he was from Iowa (known more for its pigs) and the additional fact that no one knew who his father was. Once, on one of their trips to Chicago to visit me and my sister, my mother and father brought Ming and her litter with them. The minute I laid eyes on Yanko I knew that he was not your run-of-the-mill cat. He was magical. He was so beautiful! I had seen many cats before, but he was something else—I felt like playing the piano! Right then and there, my saintly mother gave him to me and my Dominican community as a gift. We already had a cat in the community, but Yanko was different, so special, so beautiful. I literally felt like dancing when he would walk by—he was a delight!

By now you know where this is heading. Yanko was precious in that he gave me a handle on God's love for me. In the "relationship," I play God and Yanko plays me. Notice how tight the analogy is. How was it possible for someone as mighty as I, as intelligent as I, as superior as I, to fall for a lowly cat? Amazing, isn't it. Just so you don't feel tempted to call 911, a few years back a gorilla by the name of Koko appeared on the cover of *National Geographic*. What a picture that was. He was holding his pet kitty! The two cases are about the same; Koko has it over me on "mighty," I have it over him on "intelligent." Both cases make the point loud and clear: "Love" is possible even when there is a great lack of parity in being and likeness.

Another aspect of my vignette that is instructive is that personal need did not enter into the relationship—neither mine nor Yanko's. Just as God's love for us is not based on his need, so my fondness for Yanko was not based on my need. I did not need to love Yanko in order to be complete—I simply "loved" him because he was lovable. The relationship was never exclusive, never twinged with jealousy. I was even more joyful when others found him to be as fetching as I did—in fact, almost to a man, with the exception of one d-o-g person, my whole community of seven fell for Yanko. My main purpose in sharing this somewhat embarrassing "relationship" with you is to encourage you to get in touch with your own Yanko. Your Yanko might provide an even better analogy than mine if, say, your Yanko turns out to be your child. For then there would be a creative causal relationship—and this would make the analogy even closer since causality is an important aspect of the relationship between God and us.

For me, the best part of the analogy is the way it handles the problem of sin. There never was a time when I found it difficult to like Yanko—I liked him all the time. In fact, as far as I was concerned, he could do no wrong. Animals are way ahead of humans in terms of perfection. And, of course, not having free will, animals don't formally sin and are not marred by what is our biggest imperfection. One of the major differences between animals and us is that a mature animal, for the most part, is perfect, i.e., everything God had in mind when he created it. This difference between us and animals is no small difference. Imperfection in the other is the greatest obstacle we face in our attempt to love another human being. God's revelation tells us that one day each of us will be perfectly conformed to the image of Christ, i.e., perfectly lovable, but that day hasn't dawned yet. Yanko, on the other hand, was perfectly lovable in that he was perfect; he was everything that he could be. Because Yanko was perfect, I was oblivious to his behavior, not that it was all that bad. But when, for instance, he would sharpen his claws on the back of an upholstered chair, I tended to overlook it. Cats, after all, will be cats!

The Yanko affair is even more profound in addressing the question of God loving us in spite of our sins. God sees us not in the past, present, or future, but in his eternal present. We really can't wrap our minds around this concept experientially; but it means that God sees us not as we see ourselves, full of imperfection and sin, but as we will one day be—as perfect, as totally conformed to the image of his Jesus. If only we could see ourselves and others the same way that God sees us.

My relationship with the other cat deteriorated soon after Yanko came into my life. The other cat sensed that an alienation of affections was going on—a true perception. This illustrates the truism that every analogy limps—God's love is not changeable so, in this respect, my fickle behavior falls short in illustrating the universal love of God. After a few years the other cat died. Yanko, his buddy, became disconsolate and took to crying all day long, to the extent that I had to send him back to Iowa. It goes without saying that I visited him frequently. I used to say that I killed two birds with one stone in my trips: I would visit Yanko and also get a chance to see my parents. My last glimpse of Yanko was strange in the extreme. On one of my visits, immediately upon entering my boyhood home and kissing my father (my mother was already living in a nursing home), my father asked me if I wanted to see Yanko. I thought it strange that he should ask. He then went upstairs and came down carrying a shoe box with guess what inside—none other than dead Yanko. Not a great homecoming gift! Though shocked and saddened, I was relieved to hear that Yanko had died earlier that day—not sometime the week before. Yanko has been dead now for almost ten years, but he lives in my memory.

5

The Glory of the Lord Shone Around Them

There were shepherds in the region, living in the fields and keeping night watch by turns over their flocks. The angel of the Lord appeared to them as the glory of the Lord shone around them, and they were very much afraid. (Lk 2:8–9)

This year I was struck by the ordinariness of Jesus' birth. The feast of Christmas bespeaks glory, but there is precious little of it around in the gospel description of the birth of Jesus. The glory of the Lord in the passage above is the only glory to be seen with the naked eye! And this glory surrounded the shepherds—not the Christ Child. There is wall-to-wall glory in the event of Christ's birth, but it's all but invisible, seen only through the eyes of faith. I find this paradoxical in the extreme. Here we have the most prepared-for and awaited event in human history—and it is so lacking in glory that the event itself is barely noticeable. Imagine, God Almighty assumes our human nature and is born in a stable, or perhaps a cave, and laid in a manger, a trough for feeding animals! Such incongruity could come only from the hand of God.

The Church constantly reminds us of the glory, albeit invisible, of the mystery of Christmas and the Incarnation. Every prayer in the masses of Christmas mentions glory or light: "Father, you make this holy night radiant with the splendor of Jesus Christ our light" (opening prayer, first mass of Christmas). "Lord our God, with the birth of your Son, your glory breaks on the world" (alternate opening prayer, first mass of Christmas). The "glory of God" in the Jewish Scriptures was primarily a descriptor of the presence of God—mainly the presence of God in the Temple. It was a luminous cloud—I envisage it as very much like what one sees through an airplane window just before ascending above the cloud level at midday. Second Chronicles 5:14 relates that on one occasion this cloud of God's glory was so thick that the priests could not continue to minister.

The mystery of the Incarnation is dazzlingly glorious in its excess and gratuitousness. Almighty God humbles himself and takes on our human condition. I could see God becoming human for a few hours, a day perhaps—but forever? Jesus Christ, the God-man is for all eternity one of us. Not only did he assume our human nature with all its limitations and inherent weakness, but he chose to live his life in service of others—even to the extent of dying on the cross for the forgiveness of our sins. The second reading on the fourth Sunday of Advent (Heb 10:5–10) puts into Jesus' mouth the words of Psalm 40: "Behold, I come to do your will." It is clear from Jesus' words in John that doing the will of God for him consisted not so much in being obedient to God's commands, but in expressing in a visible way the heart and mind of God, i.e., God's desire to love us and even die for us if needs be. But he can't, of course, because he's God. This is the poignancy of the Incarnation. Jesus Christ, the incarnate son of God, can do just that: "He is the image of the Invisible God" (Col 1:15). This is what Hebrews 1, the second reading of the third mass of Christmas, expresses: ". . . [I]n this, the final age, he has spoken to us through his Son. . . . This Son is the . . . exact representation of the Father's being." When Jesus says, "The Father loves me for this: /that I lay down my life (Jn 10:17)," he's not talking about obedience. The Father loves Jesus for lay-ing down his life, not in that he's being obedient but in that he's expressing by that action what is in the heart and mind of God. This is the glory of God that is expressed in the Incarnation—a love beyond our ability to imagine!

When I think of my own experiences of Christmas that help to put me in touch with the lavishness of the invisible mystery of the Incarnation, two Christmases immediately come to mind—one is recent and the other occurred more than fifty years ago. My main purpose in sharing these two experiences is to encourage you to search through your own experiences of Christmas that point to the extravagance and excess in the mystery of God's love expressed in the mystery of the Incarnation. The first story is embarrassing in that the point I'm making seems so insignificant—and yet it made such an impact on me later.

Christmas 1943—what a great Christmas that was! Christmas during my childhood was always great because my parents, my sister, and I would always take the train from Iowa to visit our relatives in Kansas City. Christmas 1943 was even better than usual because my five uncles on my father's side were home on furlough. My father was the only brother who didn't serve in the military. He was the oldest and I think that his age was the reason, even though my parents told me that he was deferred so that he could take care of me—I was ten at the time and somewhat precocious. Having the uncles all back safe and sound for Christmas was such a blessing and relief, as we worried constantly about them. My Uncle Tony was on the aircraft carrier *Franklin* when it suffered a kamikaze attack several months before. He miraculously survived the blast even though his shoes were blown off his feet. The aspect, though, of Christmas 1943 which has to do with the theological point in question, the glory of the Incarnation, has no relationship to my uncles; it has to do with the Christmas tree.

It was traditional in my family to use tinsel on the tree. In 1943, tinsel, sometimes called icicles, was long strands of shiny metal about an eighth of an inch wide. Metal was very scarce during the war and to this day I don't know why it was available to us in the form of icicles. My recollection is that icicles in the forties had a large lead content—I handled enough of them to more than justify any residual attention deficit disorder. The fact of the matter was that I hated icicles—not in themselves but in the way we were forced by poverty to use them. We used them one by one. As someone once said, "We were all poor in the depression, but we didn't know it." I especially disliked the fact that at the end of the Christmas season we had to remove the icicles, one by one, and place them back into their tissue wrappings. Being fragile, they got shorter and shorter as the years went by. In my desperation, I took to throwing them at the tree. My mother would always catch me at this and make me remove every last one that I threw.

The Christmas tree of 1943 was something else again. Because of the joy of having my uncles home, my relatives went out and bought fifty packages of icicles! Imagine the splendor of picking up a whole handful and putting them *en masse* on one bough—joy and rapture unforeseen! This was the most beautiful Christmas tree in all the world—such prodigality, such excess. It was only after I became a priest that I connected that Christmas tree with the lavishness of God's love displayed in the mystery of the Incarnation.

The other Christmas of note occurred in 1989. This was when I began playing the piano for dinners and receptions at the governor's mansion in Madison, Wisconsin. My first performance was around the middle of December. There I was, playing Bach on the Steinway grand in one of the great living rooms of that grand house, trying to keep the volume at least equal to the conversation of the guests. I thought I had died and gone to heaven! After this first performance I bragged about it for three solid days until tragedy struck and I nearly cut off my right hand while sharpening a carving knife (cf. Chapter 3). I'm sure that the thought of returning to the mansion for more performances, and more to brag about, accelerated my healing and rehabilitation. I must say, though, only in recent months has my right hand felt like it belongs to me.

The mansion was wall- to-wall opulence! At Christmas, ten fifteen-foot Christmas trees were decorated—one for every room on the first floor. Each of the trees had a special theme, usually ethnic, and was exquisitely decorated with handmade ornaments. Another feature I loved during the Christmas season was the Christmas tree placed at the center of the dining room table. It was constructed of several hundred boiled shrimp which were cunningly attached by toothpicks to a Styrofoam core. All the while I was playing the piano that first time, I worried whether any shrimp would be left on the tree after I had finished playing. Mercifully, shrimp were added as needed from the infinite supply of shrimp in the kitchen. What a powerful icon that shrimp Christmas tree was. For me it represented the inexhaustible excess and glory of the mystery of Christmas, the mystery of the incarnate love of God.

6

To Each Person the Manifestation of the Spirit Is Given for the Common Good

There are different gifts but the same Spirit; there are different ministries but the same Lord; there are different works but the same God who accomplishes all of them in everyone. To each person the manifestation of the Spirit is given for the common good. To one the Spirit gives wisdom in discourse, to another the power to express knowledge. . . . But it is one and the same Spirit who produces all these gifts, distributing them to each as he wills.
(1 Cor 12:4–8, 11)

Chapters 12 and 13 of 1 Corinthians treat of grace and are extremely important theologically, because in them an important distinction is made between the two types of graces: *sanctifying grace* and what we might call *social grace*. Sanctifying grace primarily pertains to and benefits the individual, whereas social grace resides in individuals but primarily benefits the Church. This is a significant distinction and merits our consideration. Scholastic theology refers to these graces as *gratiae gratum facientes* and *gratiae gratis datae*, graces that make one holy and graces freely given.

Chapter 12 is admirable in its analogical thought and its clear teaching. There are many kinds of social graces; some are greater than others but all are necessary. And they are distributed to members of the Church as God chooses;

one person possesses one grace, another person possesses another grace—no one has them all: "God has set up in the church first apostles, second prophets, third teachers, then miracle workers, healers, assistants, administrators . . ." (1 Cor 12:28). Paul says about the same thing in Ephesians 4:11–12: "It is he who gave apostles, prophets, evangelists, pastors and teachers in roles of service for the faithful to build up the body of Christ." This lectionary translation is faulty. The revised translation is much better and reads: "And he gave some as apostles, others as prophets, others as evangelists, others as pastors and teachers, to equip the holy ones for the work for ministry." Notice the change in nuance. The latter translation is mainline Vatican II in that it asserts that all of the members of the Church (the holy ones) have a ministry, not just the bishops and priests. The ministry of the major ministers is to prepare the other members of the Church for the reception of ministerial grace. This is a sea change in our thinking. In the past, it wasn't clear whether or not anyone had ministerial graces in the Church, especially the charismatic graces. But this much was certain: If ministerial graces were to be had, they would be had by the hierarchy.

Paul then turns his attention to the diversity of members within the Church. He uses the analogy of the human body and mentions by name the head, the nose, the hands, the ears, the eyes, and the feet. In reading this, one can't help but pose the question: "What part am I?" The conclusion is that while some parts are more excellent than others, even "those members of the body which seem less important are in fact indispensable." The other side of diversity is unity: "The body is one and has many members, but all the members, many though they are, are one body" (1 Cor 12:12).

Paul then turns his attention to charity, one of the "greater gifts." Without love, all of the other gifts are for naught: "If I speak with human tongues and angelic as well, but do not have love, I am a noisy gong, a clanging cymbal" (1 Cor 13:1). A few weeks ago the Church was reading Matthew 7. I was stunned by Jesus' words: "None of those who cry out 'Lord, Lord,' will enter the kingdom of God but only the one who does the will of my Father in heaven." So far so good. But then he identifies these people. "Many will plead with me, 'Lord, Lord, have we not prophesied in your name? Have we not exorcised demons by its power? Did we not do many miracles in your name as well?' Then I will declare to them solemnly, 'I never knew you. Out of my sight, you evildoers!'" (Mt 7:21–23) What makes this passage so disconcerting is the fact that the "non-doers" are the ones we normally think of as the "doers." In fact, they are exercising the social graces of 1 Corinthians 12. Lacking in the "non-doers" are acts of love, justice and compassion—and without these, one misses the mark. So it's a question of priority; the ministerial gifts are ordered to charity. Both kinds of grace, the ministerial and the sanctifying, are important, but the sanctifying grace is more important—charity, in fact, is indispensable.

The most important part of this teaching in 1 Corinthians is that the ministerial graces are not for the individual but for the common good of the Church. This distinguishes them from the sanctifying graces which are for the individual good. Of course, individual good ultimately redounds to the societal good, just as private sin ultimately has a public effect and weakens society. It should also be pointed out that the common good, that good which is above the ability of any individual to achieve alone, is enjoyed by the individuals that make up the community. This common good distinction between the two kinds of graces must always be kept in mind because self-aggrandizement is always a temptation.

It's incumbent upon the leaders in the Church to discern ministerial gifts and to call them forth. Individuals in the Church must always keep in mind that these gifts are not for themselves but for the common good. There will always be tension with regard to this discernment. The women's ordination question is a good illustration of this tension between the charismatic and the institutional. A great deal of pain is present when one feels that his or her ministerial gifts are not being called forth or recognized. Self-aggrandizement is not necessarily at work in this situation. If I feel that God has given me a charism for a particular task in the

Church, then I will be unhappy if I am passed over for the job. In my judgment, not choosing me will jeopardize the attainment of the common good, of which I am a beneficiary. If one complains about this to the leaders, the leaders will more often than not reply that discernment of charisms is their charism. In other words, "Don't call us; we'll call you." Painful situations such as this one call for faith in God's providence and care for his church.

One of my favorite figures for illustrating charisms and the common good is the orchestra. In fact, I would say that the orchestra is a dream figure. It captures all of the points of Paul's teaching on the social graces: the common good, the fact that everyone in the Church has a gift and, finally, the unity and diversity of the Church. The mind-set of members of the symphony orchestra is very different from that of a solo performer—even if the same instrument is played in both situations. For the solo performer, the focus is on "my" individual good. For the member of the symphony, the focus is not on "me" but on the music. The music is all that matters! Whether or not I am called on to contribute to the production of the music matters little; the only important thing is the music. Some members of the orchestra appear to be playing all the time—for example, the violinists. Others, such as the harpists, play very little. I've been to performances in which the trianglist's and tympanist's combined playing time comprised less than a minute. And as for sackbutists—sometimes they don't even show up. The point of all this is, members of the orchestra don't care whether they play or not. Have you ever seen a member of the orchestra trying to get the eye of the conductor and semi-hysterically and pathetically crying out: "Use me; use me"? It just doesn't matter who's making the music, so long as it gets made. Each member of the orchestra keeps his or her eyes on the conductor and comes in when called. When one is not playing, we detect no disappointment in that member's face, just the contentment that comes from the enjoyment of good music.

In the figure, the orchestra is the Church, the audience is made up of those who don't belong to the Church, and the conductor is Jesus. I could expand on the figure a little by pointing out that the audience is getting smaller and smaller and the orchestra is getting larger and larger. The newly refurbished Orchestra Hall in Chicago now has terrace seats directly on the stage—this is where the chorus sits. I sit in these seats when I attend—and I'll probably regret saying this when I go to buy my next ticket, but they are the cheapest and best seats in the house. So far, the conductor hasn't motioned me to play anything. The goal is that ultimately the entire audience will be moved to the stage. Then there will be, in effect, no audience—God will be all in all, and all eyes will be on Jesus as he directs "a people God has made his own, to praise his glory" (Eph 1:14).

7

In My Father's House There Are Many Dwelling Places

*In my Father's house there are many
    dwelling places;
    otherwise, how could I have told you
    that I was going to prepare a place
    for you?
I am indeed going to prepare a place
    for you,
    and then I shall come back to take
    you with me,
    that where I am you also may be.
(Jn 14:2–3)*

Jesus uses "house" frequently in the gospels as a figure for heaven. Being outside the house is a figure for hell, where there is weeping and gnashing of teeth in the exterior darkness. The banquet hall is almost the same figure, and it too is used for heaven. The "many dwelling places" in the above quotation simply means that there's a lot of room in heaven. The "house" figure has always been an important figure for me.

My parents grew up within a block of each other in a Croatian enclave in Kansas City, Kansas. The place was and is called Strawberry Hill. After they married they lived with my maternal grandmother until I was born, four years later. Then they moved to Iowa—they were the only ones to move off of Strawberry Hill. My fondest memories of childhood are those involving our semi-annual train trips back to Strawberry Hill to visit all the relatives.

Those trips always remind me of "In my Father's house there are many dwelling places" for, in addition to my grandparents, there were six other family units all in that one block. My aunt and her husband lived in my mother's house. One of my father's brothers and his family lived above my father's parents. Another uncle and his family lived next door on the first floor and my aunt and her family lived next door on the second floor. Another aunt and her family lived in a house behind my grandparents and my unmarried uncle lived upstairs. I loved these visits most especially because they afforded a rare opportunity to play with all my cousins. All my grandmothers and aunts were great cooks so, all in all, going to Kansas City was like dying and going to heaven. I especially liked the fact that all these great cooks had refrigerators well stocked with fried chicken and unlimited supplies of *povitica* (Croatian pastry) and soda pop. The beauty of a ten-year-old visiting eight family units was that one could leave one house and go to another before annoyance would set in—I felt like a bee in a patch of wildflowers.

In retrospect, it surprises me that I found Strawberry Hill so attractive. It really wasn't a "house walk" neighborhood. In fact, many of the houses of Strawberry Hill in the 1940s, including my grandparents', had outhouses—two to be exact. One was a smokehouse. So much of the Hill's charm lay in the fact that this is where my family lived, hardworking people, who also knew how to celebrate life. When I say hardworking I mean "legendary" hardworking. Most of the Croats came to Strawberry Hill in the first decade of the twentieth century. They displaced the Irish and Swedes, who moved away after an unsuccessful strike in the meat packing plants. Previously the prevailing wage was eight cents per hour—my forebears were willing to work for three cents! My grandmother, in the early years of her marriage, raised six children and cooked and washed for ten borders. They were also hard playing. I'll never forget my youngest uncle's wedding. I was sixteen and privileged to be his best man. What a reception! All of the food, with the exception of the lambs, was prepared by my grandmothers and aunts: ten lambs, thirteen hams, and fifty chickens.

Several years ago I was giving a parish mission in Overland Park, Kansas. Overland Park is only about ten minutes away from Strawberry Hill. On one of the nights, I talked about Strawberry Hill as an icon of heavenly bliss. After the talk a woman came up and asked me if I knew Marijana. I said I didn't, and the woman said that I might have known her as Mary Ann Grisnik. Again I shook my head "no" but she persisted and mentioned that Marijana's maiden name was Mary Ann Pinter. Wow! Mary Ann Pinter was my childhood playmate; she lived across the street from my grandmother and her father was my father's best man.

It turned out that Marijana was a folk painter and had just had a show at the Kansas City Art Museum. On the next night my informer brought me a catalog of the show. What a precious gift that was! All of the paintings were scenes from Strawberry Hill! One of the paintings was of Mary Ann's house with Henry Mufich, the produce man, and his truck in front of my grandmother's house—Henry was my aunt-in-law's brother.

Another great picture was that of the meat market I used to go to with my grandmother for sweetbreads— imagine that, sweetbreads in a lower middle-class meat market! Marijana was on my wavelength. For her, Strawberry Hill was heaven, and I felt the same way. My favorite painting of hers is more symbolic; it depicts angels from heaven descending on Strawberry Hill carrying the sacred *povitica*—a walnut and honey strudel that is the national dessert of Croatia. I could go on and on. The catalog contains about thirty pictures—each one greater than the previous one. What a treasure this book has been for me. Just imagine having a book filled with pictures of heaven.

I can't overemphasize the importance of having icons of heaven, such as Strawberry Hill, and I encourage you to uncover similar ones from your life experience. Belief in resurrection of the body is an essential Christian belief. Recently I've been running into Christians who don't believe in resurrection; they think that they're going to be disembodied spirits after they die. The New Testament is absolutely clear on the resurrection from the dead: "Death came through a man: hence the resurrection of the dead comes through a man also. Just as in Adam all die, so in Christ all will come to life again, but each one in proper order: Christ the first fruits and then, at his coming, all those who belong to him" (1 Cor 15: 21–23). It couldn't be stated more clearly. The verses immediately before these are also interesting: "If Christ was not raised, your faith is worthless. You are still in your sins, and those who have fallen asleep in Christ are the deadest of the dead. If our hopes in Christ are limited to this life only, we are the most pitiable of men" (1 Cor 15:17–19). These words are intriguing. They make it clear that being a Christian sets us apart from others in that the life of a Christian is extraordinarily difficult. In Romans 12, we are enjoined to avoid the *carpe diem* mentality of the world: "Do not conform yourselves to this age but be transformed." In other words: "Clothe yourselves with heartfelt mercy, with kindness, humility, meekness, and patience" (Col 3:12). Jesus himself warns us: "Whoever wishes to be my follower must deny his very self, take up his cross each day and follow in my steps" (Lk 9:23). This is why we would be more pitiable if there is no resurrection from the dead. It would be a case of unrealized delayed gratification. It's hard to imagine what resurrected life will be like, but images such as Strawberry Hill help to sharpen our appetites for life on high with Jesus and with all the members of our families who have gone before us.

8

Unless the Grain of Wheat Falls to the Earth and Dies

I solemnly assure you,
unless the grain of wheat falls to the
earth and dies,
it remains just a grain of wheat.
But if it dies,
it produces much fruit. (Jn 12:24)

In John 16:7 Jesus tells his disciples: "Yet I tell you the sober truth: / It is much better for you that I go. / If I fail to go / the Paraclete will never come to you, / whereas if I go, / I will send him to you." This is a surprising statement, indeed! How can it be better for us if Jesus goes away? I'm sure his disciples were as puzzled by these words as we are. After thinking about this verse for many years, I've come to the conclusion that three things happened after Jesus went away that make our situation now better than it would have been if he had remained with us—and each of them has to do with a particular aspect of grace. In this chapter I'll consider only one of the ways. I would consider the other two, but they're not figures—therefore I'll leave you with the homework assignment of discovering the other two on your own.

"But if it dies, it produces much fruit." The "fruit" is one of the three reasons it's better now that Jesus has gone. Through grace we become that abundant fruit. Notice that the figure of fruit here in John 12 is totally different from that of John 15. In John 15 the figure means apostolic work, especially intercessory prayer. The figure is masterful in its clarity and simplicity. Jesus uses wheat as the analogue. It won't do any harm if I change the figure to corn and, besides, coming from Iowa, I know a lot more about corn than I do about wheat. Absolutely speaking, I know precious little about corn since I grew up in town, not on a farm. I do know enough, though, to earn a little extra "garage sale" money betting on the question: "How many ears of corn does one kernel produce?" The average person answers "Two." "One" is the correct answer. When I was growing up, eighty bushels to the acre was the norm; now, because the plants are so close together, the average yield is almost double that!

The beauty of the figure lies in the fact that the kernels that are produced are identical to the original kernel that was planted. Another striking aspect of the figure is the abundance of the kernels that come from the one that was planted. Several years ago I took a very chic fashion photo of my parents. I took them to the Farmers Cooperative in their hometown for the picture. It was harvest time, and that year was especially abundant. Consequently, there was not enough room to put all the corn in the cement bins of the grain elevator. Instead, it was piled on a plastic liner on top of the ground. What a sight that was! That corn pyramid rivaled the pyramids of Egypt. I took several pictures with my parents standing in front of their 1965 robin's egg blue Imperial hardtop—the corn pyramid in the background. It's too bad the year was 1990—that picture, if I had taken it in 1965 and sold it to Chrysler, would have sold a lot of Imperials. We are the kernels that make up the corn pyramid—billions of us down through the last twenty centuries. And we all come from that one kernel of corn that "fell to the earth and died."

"If it dies, it produces much fruit." In other words, "I will duplicate myself in you." It's very hard for us to believe that the Spirit of Jesus makes us like Jesus. In Galatians, Paul says: "God has sent forth into our hearts the spirit of his Son which cries out 'Abba!'" He refers to the "spirit of his Son," not so much because the Spirit comes from the Son, but because the Spirit is a Son-producing spirit. Only Jesus could address God as "Abba." Therefore we must become like Jesus before we address God as "Abba." We like to think that the divinity of Jesus, the *hypostatic union* (union between the divine and human natures of Christ in one person), is the reason why Jesus is so good and attractive as a human being. This is not the case—his divinity is totally hidden. His goodness and attractiveness come from grace—the very grace that he shares with us through the Holy Spirit, his Spirit. What made Jesus good and attractive is within us; we are very much like him. We like to "pedestalize" Jesus—the higher we place him, the more comfortable we can be with our own mediocrity and lackluster. But the facts are otherwise; grace has raised us up too. "Both with and in Christ Jesus he raised us up and gave us a place in the heavens"(Eph 2:6).

There used to be a program on TV called *To Tell the Truth*. I missed most of the episodes of that program because as a Dominican clerical brother I was not allowed to watch television—oh, how I miss the good old days! The few episodes I did see were to my liking, and I've always had the fantasy of having Jesus appear on that program with two fakes. For fakes I would invite St. Dominic and St. Francis. Do you think you'd be able to tell who's the real Jesus? Of course, St. Dominic would not be wearing black and white, and St. Francis would not be wearing brown. All three would be wearing "Jesus-like" clothes. All three would look like Jesus, talk like Jesus, and act like Jesus. My fantasy of fantasies would be for the studio audience to deem Jesus an impostor and pick one of the others as the genuine Jesus. Would Jesus then throw a tantrum and start a fight with St. Dominic, the people's choice? (I'm only kidding about that—St. Francis always has been and always will be more popular than St. Dominic.) No, not at all; he would be more than happy. He would be thrilled, in fact, knowing that he hadn't died in vain.

The breathtaking remake that God does on us through the grace of Christ flows from his love for us. Jesus reveals the stupendous love that the Father has for us in John 17:23: "So shall the world know that you sent me, / and that you loved them as you loved me." The "as" here means "to the degree that." This revelation is hard to believe! A little imaginative scene might help here. Imagine that you are seven years old and that you and your classmates are celebrating a birthday at the Buffalo—the Buffalo, which used to be at Irving Park and Pulaski, was one of the Chicago's most famous ice cream parlors. It was "turn-of-the-century" with a tin ceiling, round tables with wire chairs, and a marble floor. The marble fountain had big handles for the soda and phosphates, and had more than enough revolving stools for you and your entire class. Imagine that you and your friends are sitting at the fountain. The soda jerk starts at his left and goes from left to right, one by one, asking: "What would you like today, Sunshine." I need to provide two other points of information: One of your classmates is Jesus, and the soda jerk is, *salva reverentia*, God, the Father. This whole scene is being video taped by your parents—they came along as chaperones and van drivers. The big question now has to do with that video tape. If you sent it to me later on, in watching it, would I be able to tell which one of the little tykes is Jesus? Would I notice that the soda jerk is treating one of the children more tenderly and with greater affection than the others? In other words, from the video tape would I be able to single out Jesus? The kid next to you tells the soda jerk that he would like a banana split. The soda jerk replies: "Coming right up." When the soda jerk asks you what you'd like, you say: "I'd like to have a chocolate malt, so thick that you can stand a spoon up in it." What does he say? "Coming right up," or "How about a small scoop of vanilla?" I'm sure he'd say: "Coming right up." That's the point—there's no differentiation! In other words, the kid with the banana split is not necessarily Jesus. It's the gospel truth—God does love you and all the other kids as he loves his Jesus. "See what love the Father has bestowed on us / in letting us be called children of God! / Yet that is what we are" (1 Jn 3:1).

9

My Father Has Been Glorified in Your Bearing Much Fruit

It was not you who chose me,
it was I who chose you
to go forth and bear fruit.
Your fruit must endure,
so that all you ask the Father
in my name
he will give you. . . .
On that day you will ask in my name
and I do not say
that I will petition the
Father for you.
The Father already loves you. . . .
(Jn 15:16, 16:26–27)

The above passage is laden with revelatory fruit and will give us much to contemplate. The figure of "fruit" is an easy figure to visualize. Jesus uses "fruit" also in John 12:24 but in a completely different way (cf. Chapter 8). Once, while giving a talk on this passage, I found out that the adult audience had totally misconstrued Jesus' use of the figure. Almost everyone thought that to "Go forth and bear fruit" meant the same as "Be fertile and multiply" (Gen 1:28)—in other words, "Go forth and have children." Here the context is not children but the prayer of petition, intercessory prayer.

When we think of the prayer of petition, two problems immediately come to mind. The first is sizable: When we pray, we don't change the will of God. The second is almost as large: There doesn't seem to be proportionality between the act of praying and the petitioned effect. Who we are and what we do in prayer don't seem to measure up to the prayed-for effect. If we don't change God's will, then won't the same results unfold in time whether we pray for them or not? Here we encounter the awesome mystery of free will as it interfaces with God's will. St. Thomas answers this question by saying that some things are in God's will contingently, i.e., only on condition that we pray for them. The answer is more mysterious than the problem, for it implies that God is able to move the human will, all the while preserving the will's freedom. Since we don't change the will of God, the first requisite is that we pray according to the will of God. This is somewhat limiting and is not always easy to discern. Tommy Tyson, the famous Methodist evangelist, is fond of saying: "When we pray we need sensitivity akin to that needed when sitting on a dime and being able to tell whether it's heads or tails."

St. Thomas in his *Summa* addresses the subject of praying for those things which are in the ambit of God's will. He teaches that if four conditions are present, prayer will be infallible. The conditions are that the prayer be 1) pious, 2) persevering, 3) for one's self and, finally, 4) for something ordered to one's salvation. Condition three greatly limits the scope of infallible prayer, but it is a necessary condition because of free will—another person's salvation depends on that person's freely chosen will to cooperate with God's grace. Condition four might possibly be the reason you didn't win at Power Ball last week. In a more positive vein, condition 4 follows from the revelation of God's universal salvific will. "I urge that petitions, prayers, intercession, and thanksgiving be offered for all. . . . Prayer of this kind is good, and God our savior is pleased with it, for he wants all . . . to be saved and come to know the truth" (1 Tim 2:1, 3). The bottom line of this teaching is that you will be saved if you pray for your salvation—an extremely comforting conclusion for all of us, especially for those who have serious doubts about this matter.

With regard to prayer for others, our prayer can still be infallible if we know for certain that we're praying for something that God wants. However, God's specific will, as opposed to his general will, is not easy to discern. It can only be known through prayer; therefore a good percentage of our prayer for others must consist of praying for knowledge concerning the object of our prayer.

Sometimes suffering enters into intercessory prayer. When it does, it's either there as a part of the process of determining exactly for whom and/or for what God wants us to pray, or as the prayer itself: "Even now I find my joy in the suffering I endure for you. In my own flesh I fill up what is lacking in the sufferings of Christ for the sake of his body, the church" (Col 1:24).

Several years ago, *Masterpiece Theatre* presented a great story entitled: *Reilly, Ace of Spies*. It was about Sidney Reilly, the most celebrated spy of the early twentieth century. One episode was especially interesting to me in that it revealed that Caryll Houselander was his lover. The affair ended after Caryll returned to the practice of Catholicism, but they remained friends. One especially poignant series of scenes switched back and forth between Sidney, in a Bolshevik prison awaiting execution, and Caryll, suffering excruciating pain in a London hospital. At the exact moment that the firing squad's bullet found its mark, the scene switched back to Caryll in her hospital bed. In that instant, her pain came to a sudden end. The implication was that she was suffering vicariously for Sidney's spiritual well-being. Imagine that—high theology on *Masterpiece Theatre*. Later on I found all of this in Maisie Ward's biography of Caryll.

Vicarious suffering plays a major role in most of our serious illnesses, whether we are aware or not. In fact, the main effects of the sacrament of anointing of the sick are grace—first of all, to strengthen the soul against fear and despair and, second, grace to produce that generosity which enables the sick person to conjoin his or her suffering to that of Christ for the sake of his body, the Church.

The life of St. Dominic is very illustrative in this regard. He was preeminently a preacher, but he was also a man of prayer, especially intercessory prayer. Dominic spent a good portion of his nights interceding for sinners—in fact, he spent as much time in intercessory prayer as he did in preaching.

In the beginning quotation from John, Jesus speaks of "praying in my name." A correct understanding of this phrase is essential to the ministry of intercessory prayer. In general, we tend to interpret these words in a minimalist way, as does the Church in her liturgical prayers. Prayers usually end with "through our Lord Jesus Christ. . . ." This is "praying in the name of Jesus" in the sense of using spiritual "clout." I'm not critical of the practice, but it's not what Jesus has in mind in John 16:26–27: "On that day you will ask in my name, / and I do not say that I will petition the Father for you. / The Father already loves you. . . ." Here Jesus is using "in my name" in the way he uses it in the Great Commandment of Matthew 28: "Baptize them in the name / 'of the Father, / and of the Son, / and of the Holy Spirit,'" i.e., in the *power* of the Trinity. To pray in the name of Jesus is to pray in the power of Jesus—in other words, to come before God, as Jesus, as God's beloved. Here we touch the sublime mystery of grace, that sanctifying grace which transforms us into the image of Jesus. When Jesus prays for us in John 17:20 ("I pray also for those who will believe in me through their word"), we never have reason to doubt the efficacy of his prayer. We don't have a problem with proportionality when Jesus is praying. Why? Because it's Jesus doing the praying. But when we pray it's a different story: "I and my prayers are puny indeed in the sight of God." Nothing could be further from the truth. The revelation of "in my name" is that in God's sight our prayers are about the same as those of Jesus! He hears us because, like Jesus, we are precious in his eyes. When we pray we can even dare to say to God: "Look at me and hear me. I am your Jesus."

A few words concerning technique in prayer. There's a fresco by Fra Angelico on one of the walls in the cloister garden of San Marco in Florence. It shows St. Dominic embracing the feet of the crucified Jesus. Sometimes, when I pray for someone, I imagine that person before the crucifix in the posture of Dominic. Sometimes I imagine myself bringing that person to the foot of the cross and presenting him or her to Jesus. Of course, there are many other ways of actually praying. It's important to note that technique isn't important. Often we think that some are gifted in intercessory prayer. The only giftedness here is the will to pray for others and the discernment of the "for whom" and the "for what."

It's interesting to note that whenever Jesus mentions "fruit" in John 15, he means the product of apostolic labor, and the reference is always to intercessory prayer. In other words, ministerial fruit, *par excellence*, is intercessory prayer. This, therefore, is of great practical import. It is ironic, but just think of it: When you retire you'll have more time to devote to intercessory prayer. You'll have more time to produce the real fruit: "If you live in me, / and my words stay part of you, / you may ask what you will— / it will be done for you. / My Father has been glorified / in your bearing much fruit" (Jn 15:7–8).

10

You Will See the Angels of God Ascending and Descending on the Son of Man

Philip sought out Nathanael and told him, "We have found the one Moses spoke of in the law—the prophets too—Jesus, son of Joseph, from Nazareth." Nathanael's response to that was, "Can anything good come from Nazareth?" and Philip replied, "Come, see for yourself." When Jesus saw Nathanael coming toward him, he remarked: "This man is a true Israelite. There is no guile in him." "How do you know me?" Nathanael asked him. "Before Philip called you," Jesus answered, "I saw you under the fig tree." "Rabbi," said Nathanael, "you are the Son of God; you are the king of Israel." Jesus responded: "Do you believe just because I told you I saw you under the fig tree? You will see much greater things than that." He went on to tell them, "I solemnly assure you, you shall see the sky opened and the angels of God ascending and descending on the Son of Man." (Jn 1:45–51)

As an introduction to the above Scripture quote, I want to turn our attention to sacrifice. Sacrifice, though a very primitive religious practice and occurring throughout the pages of the Old Testament, is still, in its sacramental non-physical form, very much a part of Catholic practice. The mass can be seen from many viewpoints, but its sacrificial aspect is the most important. In sacrifice, a precious gift of God, preferably an animal, is destroyed or killed in symbolic recognition of God's absolute preeminence and sovereignty over all of creation and especially over one's life. *Sacrifice* is an external physical action and is ultimately intended to lead to the internal spirituality of worship. *Worship* is an act of one's will by which one tells God: "You created me, you have supreme dominion over my life, you are Lord, I belong to you, do with me what you will." Worship of God along with love of God is the most perfect of human acts. Nonetheless, sacrifice currently suffers very bad press—those who sacrifice chickens in their backyards very quickly become social pariahs. The sacrifice of the mass escapes bad public press precisely because it is a true sacrifice but not a physical and bloody sacrifice. The sacrificial aspect of the mass is symbolized by the double consecration of bread and wine. Separate elements of bread and wine bespeak the separation of Jesus' blood from his body—a separation which ordinarily implies death.

Bad press also currently applies to the idea of *lordship*— even when the reference is to God. Ours is a culture which idolizes freedom and eschews all forms of dominion and lordship. It's annoying but somewhat comical to find passages in the Bible which have substituted the word "God" for "Lord." The ostensible reason for such circumlocution is the avoidance of sexist language, but an even greater albeit subconscious reason is that the very notion of dominion over another, even God's dominion over his creation, is disdained.

Priesthood, in general, is the ability to offer sacrifice. In the Church there are two forms of priesthood. Both of them participate in *the* priesthood, the priesthood of Christ. They are the common priesthood and the ordained priesthood. Christ's priesthood began with the first moment of his human life and culminated in his sacrifice at Golgotha. In this bloody sacrifice, Christ, as priest and as representative of humanity, offered and gave himself as victim to God (the Father by attribution) in acknowledgment of God's sovereign dominion over all of creation. Christ continues to offer this sacrifice in an unbloody manner in his Church through the ministry of the ordained. The ordained priest is enabled by the character of holy orders to be the instrument by which Christ exercises sacramentally, in the consecration of the mass, the sacrifice which he made of himself on the cross. The common priesthood is an enabling, by means of the characters of baptism and confirmation, which allows one to make his or her own sacrifice of Golgotha which Christ, by means of the ordained priesthood, actualizes sacramentally in the mass. In making this religious sacrifice, each of us is thus able to offer his or her very life back to God.

The two kinds of priesthood are distinct and cannot be ranked. Both are essential to the life of the Church. In some respects, the ordained priesthood is more important—there could be no mass without the exercise of the ordained priest's instrumental powers. But in other ways, the common priesthood is more important because when an ordained priest says mass, he is also obligated to exercise his common priesthood. Otherwise he personally offers offense to God, not worship.

Back to the opening quotation from John. The quotation is interesting on many counts. One is that it gives us a between-the-lines insight into Jesus' thought processes. He perceives Nathanael as a person without guile and calls him a true Israelite. This triggers thoughts about Israel [Jacob] who was full of guile. And these thoughts trigger in Jesus' mind one of the most striking images in the story of Jacob, the image of Jacob's ladder: "You shall see . . . the angels of God ascending and descending on the Son of Man." This is a clear reference to Genesis 28:12: "Then he [Jacob] had a dream: a stairway rested on the ground, with its top reaching to the heavens; and God's messengers were going up and down on it." (Most commentators say that the stairway was a ziggurat, a Mesopotamian temple similar to the Mayan temples in Central America.) The meaning of the figure in Genesis is obscure, but this is not the case in John. Jesus clearly identifies himself as Jacob's ladder— what a tremendous theological metaphor! In other words, Jesus is the nexus between heaven and earth: "One also is the mediator between God and men, / the man Christ Jesus" (1 Tim 2:5). I especially like "the angels of God ascending and descending on the Son of Man." "Angels" here doesn't refer to real angels but to commerce, divine and human commerce, briskly taking place through Jesus, the link between heaven and earth. Jesus, from the first moment of his existence as a human being, was and is high priest. He continually offers sacrifice to God on our behalf and brings back from heaven God's blessing and grace. He is the one mediator between heaven and earth.

This brings to mind another metaphor from childhood. The J. C. Penney store in my hometown of Creston, Iowa, had fast-moving overhead cables on pulleys that carried all the currency that was exchanged in the store. To this day, I don't know why individual clerks didn't have access to cash registers on the main floor of the store. Perhaps the cable system was more economical, perhaps the clerks couldn't be trusted—highly unlikely in the forties and fifties. Anyway, the cable system was the medium for all commerce. The clerks put the money into a screw-top container, attached it to the staging mechanism, pulled a lever, and off went the money up to the balcony—all thanks to the cable system. There change would be made and sent back on the return cable. Jesus is the J. C. Penney cable system! He takes our worship up to God and brings back God's grace and our sanctification.

At this point it would be well to quote Cyprian Vaggagini's definition of liturgy. Liturgy is a "complexus of sensible signs by means of which God, in Christ and through Christ, in the Church and through the Church, sanctifies man, and man, in Christ and through Christ, in the Church and through the Church, renders worship to God."

Notice how similar are the metaphors and Vaggagini's definition of liturgy. The mass is *par excellence* liturgy. And in the mass, Jesus the high priest re-presents and makes present the sacrifice of the cross. Through the empowerment that is part of the grace of baptism, the "priesthood of all believers," all of the baptized who attend mass, are able to join with Jesus in offering to the Father the sacrifice of sacrifices, namely Jesus himself who is at one and the same time priest and victim.

What a tremendous privilege it is to be able to join with Jesus in offering him and ourselves to God. As with all privileges, though, there is also an obligation. We must really join in! We must really worship God. If we choose not to offer ourselves at mass, we would be better off not attending. We must remember what worship connotes: the absolute dominion of God over one's life. If worship is the willingness to give back to God one's life, if needs be, *a fortiori*, we must also be willing to give up all that we are holding in our hands—that includes our sins, our unforgiveness, our excessive attachment to creatures and self. You can see what a powerful means the sacrifice of the mass can be for spiritual growth. If we fully participate, we offer ourselves to God—lock, stock, and barrel. There is no better, more powerful way of getting closer to God.

A valuable comparison can be made between participating in worship and making the solemn vows of the religious state. St. Thomas teaches that the act of taking the solemn vows of religion results in the total remission of one's sins. In entering the religious state, one receives the same grace as one receives in baptism. This is because in making solemn vows, one places one's self totally at God's service (*ST*, 2a2ae, 189.3). Notice how similar this is to worship. This is the goal of Christian life, to place one's self entirely in God's service. We can do this at mass because Jesus, the sole mediator between heaven and earth, Jacob's ladder, takes our worship up to heaven and returns with additional grace by which we are "transformed from glory to glory into his very image" (2 Cor 3:18).

11

All That the Lord Has Said, We Will Heed and Do

"Bring me a three-year-old heifer, a three-year-old she-goat, a three-year-old ram, a turtledove, and a young pigeon." He brought him all these, split them in two, and placed each half opposite the other; but the birds he did not cut up. . . . When the sun had set and it was dark, there appeared a smoking brazier and a flaming torch, which passed between those pieces.
(Gen 15:9–10,17)

When Moses came to the people and related all the words of the Lord, they all answered with one voice:

"We will do everything that the LORD has told us." . . . Then, having sent certain young men of the Israelites to offer holocaust and sacrifice young bulls as peace offerings to the LORD. Moses took half of the blood and put it in large bowls; the other half he splashed on the altar. Taking the book of the covenant, he read it aloud to the people, who answered. "All that the LORD has said, we will heed and do." Then he took the blood and sprinkled it on the people, saying, "This is the blood of the covenant which the LORD has made with you."
(Ex 24:3, 5–7)

In this chapter we'll look at Eucharist *qua* covenant and examine two covenant figures from the Jewish Scriptures. These figures are, to my mind, the most striking in the Scriptures—unforgettable in their graphic and gory detail. Eucharist, without doubt, has a covenantal aspect, and these figures will assist us in no small way when we attend mass.

The first figure occurs in Genesis 15 and has to do with the ratification of the covenant God made with Abraham. Biblical covenants are solemn contracts or agreements and are either unilateral or bilateral. Both the figures of this chapter pertain to bilateral covenants. In Genesis 15, God, on his part, promises that Abram's natural descendants will be as numerous as the stars in the sky. Abram, on his part, "put his faith in the Lord." This doesn't sound like much of an obligation, but given his advanced age, Abram's faith was heroic and required his going far out on the limb of trust. In Romans 4:3–5, St. Paul makes reference to Abram's faith in the context of faith and justification.

The ratification of this covenant contains hidden humor, probably unintentional. What strikes my funny bone is the matter-of-fact narration of the splitting of the animals. Although most of my relatives worked in the meat-packing houses of Kansas City, I only experienced the slaughtering of a steer once, and in Iowa. It was awesome and bloody—there was more blood than one could imagine. In this vignette one gets the impression that the splitting of the heifer took no time at all, but with the tools that were available in Abram's day, the task must have taken the better part of a week. The fact that the birds were not split in two also strikes me as humorous. I haven't personally cut in two any pigeons, but I imagine that I'd end up with mostly feathers—all over the place.

The smoking brazier and flaming torch of verse 17 are the most important part of the figure. They represent God and Abram walking through the carcasses. I must make an aside here. In Dominican houses it used to be the custom, until a few years ago, to have reading during meals. On one occasion, one of my classmates was the reader. When he came to verse 17 he confused "brazier" with another similar-sounding word—that ended the reading and the silence for that meal. God and Abram walking through the carcasses represents their commitment to the solemn contract: "Let happen to me what happened to these animals if I do not live up to my part of the agreement." What a practical video for us to contemplate as we attend mass. If we keep in mind the sentiments Abram had as he walked through the animals, how can we fail to grow in holiness? When we first walked through, at our baptism, most of us were not really conscious. Each time we attend mass we have the opportunity to walk through again, with greater and greater determination.

The second figure involves the ratification of the covenant God made with the people through Moses. This covenant involved the people's assent to the Ten Commandments, which were as yet unwritten. Notice that the people give their assent before the ratification: "We will do everything that the LORD has told us." The use of blood here is unforgettable. I often fantasize about reenacting this scene during mass—that would truly be a sermon not soon forgotten! The only thing that holds me back is that dry-cleaning bill—also the possibility of someone calling 911. Imagine it: Moses takes half of the blood and throws it against the altar. Next, he takes the other half and throws it on the people. My text reads "sprinkled"—much too tentative and polite. The Revised Standard Version reads "throws." This figure is astonishing in its shocking simplicity. The altar represents God. Therefore the blood, which touches the altar and the people, unites God and the people.

Notice that the covenantal aspect of Eucharist is similar to the sacrificial aspect. Both aspects require great generosity. In sacrifice we acknowledge that God is lord of all creation and we, in a sense, give our lives completely back to him. In covenant we also acknowledge the lordship of God: "All that the LORD has said, we will heed and do." Mass is the time *par excellence* to renew our baptismal covenant. Here again, it must be noted that if one comes to mass unwilling to renew that covenant first made at baptism, that person sins.

Jesus alludes to the ratification of the Mosaic covenant in the words he spoke at the Last Supper: "Then he took a cup, and after giving thanks he gave it to them, saying, 'Drink from it, all of you; for this is my blood of the covenant, which is poured out for many for the forgiveness of sins'" (Mt 26:27–28). Revelation doesn't get better than this. Here Jesus proclaims that his blood will replace the animal blood of the old covenant. His blood is the new nexus between God and his people. Hebrews 13:20 refers to the blood of Jesus as the blood of the "eternal covenant." Jesus' blood is the new glue that forever joins God with us. If we come to mass armed with this thought, how can we fail to give ourselves completely to God? How can we fail to ratify, in a new and deeper way, the covenant of our baptism?

St. Paul, in 2 Corinthians, presents some interesting "revisionist" teaching on the difference between the old and new covenants. Conventional wisdom has it that Moses wore a veil over his face to protect the people from the blinding brilliance of his face. After talking with God face to face, or perhaps face to back (Ex 33:23), his face shone with the glory of God, and he wore a veil so as not to frighten off the people. An aside is appropriate here. The Hebrew verb for "to be radiant" is the same as the Hebrew noun meaning "horn." St. Jerome, alas, mistranslated the word as he was writing the *Vulgate*—this is the reason that Michelangelo's *Moses* has horns coming out of his head. Anyway, Paul has another interpretation for the veil: "Moses . . . used to hide his face with a veil so that the Israelites could not see the final fading of the glory" (2 Cor 3:13). In other words, the radiance of his face diminished with time, and the veil saved Moses from embarrassment. Paul then compares the fading of Moses' face to the new covenant. The old covenant was a fading covenant, while the new covenant only grows brighter with time. "All of us, gazing on the Lord's glory with unveiled faces, are being transformed from glory to glory into his very image by the Lord who is the Spirit" (2 Cor 3:18).

12

Which of You Would Hand His Son a Stone?

Ask and you will receive. Seek and you will find. Knock, and it will be opened to you. For the one who asks, receives. The one who seeks, finds. The one who knocks, enters. Would one of you hand his son a stone when he asks for a loaf, or a poisonous snake when he asks for a fish? If you, with all your sins, know how to give your children what is good, how much more will your heavenly Father give good things to anyone who asks him! (Mt 7:7–11)

This teaching of Jesus on petitionary prayer contains one of the truly great biblical figures: God is *Our Father*. The figure is succinct, clear, and striking—striking because of the power of its, *a fortiori*, argumentation.

Before we turn to the figure, a review of Chapter 9 on prayer may be in order because prayer is a difficult and mysterious reality to contemplate. Two problems surround it: the problem of proportionality and the problem of God's immutable will. In his teaching, Jesus bypasses both of these problems and moves directly to the stunning bottom line: Just as fathers give their children that for which they ask, all the more will our heavenly Father give us what we ask of him. Why? Because he's better than our natural fathers—he's a super dad!

It's a shame that "father" has fallen on hard times in recent years. A significant number of people now recoil when they hear the word "father" because for them the word bespeaks gender repression and domination, or brings back painful memories from childhood of a neglectful or abusive father. What is somewhat perplexing about this phenomenon is that "mother" retains its untarnished "apple pie" status even though many, though not as many, harbor memories from childhood of a neglectful or abusive mother. Thirty years ago both words were universally cherished—certainly this was the case when Jesus used the figure of "father" for God. Given the difficulties many have with "father" today, perhaps future translations of the passage should give the reader an option and use the word "mother/father."

When I apply Jesus' figure to my own experience, two fathers come to mind: my own and the father of one of my childhood friends. I ask in advance that you not make fun of me, for the vignette I'm about to share seems trivial now, sixty years later, but one of my fondest childhood memories has to do with my father as chef—ironic, because he was not a chef. My mother wore the kitchen apron in the family.

Every Sunday my father, my sister, and I used to engage in a solemn ritual. The three of us would get up early and proceed immediately to the living room sofa with the Sunday paper in hand. There my sister and I would sit on either side of my father, laughing to our hearts' content, as he read us the funnies from beginning to end. For me this was quality time, the highlight of my week. Afterwards we would have breakfast. The breakfast was always the same and each time my father would "prepare" it. Breakfast consisted of a loaf of Harvest Bread toast stacked on a plate in the middle of the kitchen table. The part that impressed my impressionable five-year-old mind was all the butter that my father used to slather the toast—the sight of all that butter running down the mountainsides was almost too much to take in. The experience was akin to dying and going to heaven, because this was something that my mother would definitely not have allowed had she been awake. Even then, before it was fashionable, my mother was extremely health conscious—couple that interest with my sister's tendency—and mine—to be on the "pleasingly plump" side, and you have a childhood without a lot of butter running down slathered toast—at least not on weekdays.

During these breakfast orgies my father came across to me as one generous and loving father. That buttered toast for me was the epitome of fatherly love, prodigality and largesse. What a boon these childhood breakfasts have been for me in my prayer life—if my father could be so kind and loving as to provide all that buttered toast, what can I expect from Our Father. Now that I'm a bit older, the toast, of course, has lost its appeal. Nevertheless, the image is still powerful; all I have to do is change the menu from toast to eggs Benedict.

The other father from my childhood who vividly illustrates Jesus' teaching on prayer is the father of my childhood friend and classmate, Nicky. When I think of doting, extra generous fathers, Nicky's father wins hands down. He also complements the image I have of my father as I reflect on Jesus' teaching. It's not that my father wasn't kind and loving—all that toast proves that he was. It's rather that Nicky's father was kind and loving *and* rich. This is not meant in any way to fault my father. In the Depression we were all poor—we just didn't know it. Or, to be more accurate, we were all poor except for Nicky and his family. I was told that Nicky's father made his fortune by buying a lot of inexpensive land out West that eventually was found to be full of shale.

So Nicky's father was rich as well as kind. He was able to buy Nicky whatever he wanted—like electric trains. To this day I suffer from PTSS (post-traumatic stress syndrome) which I incurred from never getting the electric train that I wanted in the worst way for many a Christmas. My parents' priorities were all wrong. Granted, they were of limited means, but they could have come up with the money. It's just that they chose to invest in piano lessons rather than in my electric train! Nicky, on the other hand, had more trains than he could keep track of. One Christmas he got a train that took up most of the first floor of their house—I'm not exaggerating! It was almost large enough for him to ride on.

Nicky's father provides me with the power side of the father figure. Not only was he kind, but he had the resources he needed to be generous to a fault—in this latter respect he's like our heavenly Father who is kind and loving and, above all, has the wherewithal to give lavish gifts to his children.

Growing up with a rich playmate in the Depression was a memorable and unique experience. Being rich, Nicky was into toys of every sort, especially mechanical toys. One of his interests was model airplanes. I was also interested, but Nicky had ten airplanes for every one of mine. I believe I had one. His planes were ten times larger than mine, and his had gasoline engines! His planes actually flew! One incident involving one of his planes clearly separated the men from the boys. It occurred one summer day right after he had finished constructing one of his planes. This one was the most beautiful I had ever seen. Its wingspan must have been about four feet. Beautiful as it was, its maiden flight made an even greater impression on me. Nicky started the plane's propeller but before he let go of it, he pulled out his father's silver cigarette lighter from his pocket and set fire to the fuselage. The plane went up in a blaze of glory never to return. As the saying goes: "When you've got it, Baby, flaunt it!"

Perhaps Nicky's father was a little too doting, a little too generous. But if one abstracts from these excesses, he remains a great illustration of what Jesus is teaching us about our heavenly Father and his relationship with his petitioning children. He's powerful, loving, and generous to a fault. Nicky's father, my father, and fathers like yours, I hope, image our heavenly Father. Would one of you hand his son a stone when he asks for a loaf of slathered toast?

13

I Myself Am the Living Bread

I myself am the bread of life.
No one who comes to me
*   shall ever be hungry,*
no one who believes in me
*   shall ever thirst. . . .*
He who feeds on my flesh
and drinks my blood
has life eternal
and I will raise him up on the last day.
For my flesh is real food
and my blood real drink.
(Jn 6: 35, 54–55)

Jesus uses the figure of bread in John 6:32–58. In verses 32–51 Jesus applies the figure to himself *per se;* in verses 52–58 he applies the figure to himself as Eucharist. This is an important point because we miss a lot if we think of the entire passage as eucharistic. Jesus refers to himself as bread coming down from heaven. He distinguishes between two breads coming down from heaven: the manna given by Moses, and himself, the real heavenly bread given by the Father. "I myself am the bread of life." The "the" here is crucial. As in "I am the good shepherd," the "the" means "genuine" and "only." Therefore the verse means: "I am the only bread of life—all others are ersatz compared to me."

"God's bread comes down from heaven / and gives life to the world . . . / I myself am the bread of life" (Jn 6:33–35). Here Jesus is talking about himself *per se*, not *qua* eucharist.

The life-giving aspect of food is paramount here. The next verse is extremely important: "No one who comes to me shall ever be hungry, no one who believes in me shall ever thirst." There's Jewish parallelism here: "Comes to me" is synonymous with "believes in me." In other words, we eat the life-giving bread, which is Jesus, by believing in him. Notice how whole and complete the metaphor is, without any reference, direct or implied, to Eucharist. Contemplation of this powerful metaphor can only increase one's union with Christ. By faith in Jesus we are united with him and share in his life.

In verse 52 Jesus changes gears and begins to use the metaphor to describe himself as Eucharist. I find it extremely interesting that "bread" is not mentioned again until verse 58. In verses 52 to 57 "flesh" replaces "bread." This is entirely to my liking because I find "bread" to be a weak figure in Western culture of the late twentieth century. When I think of life-giving food I don't think of bread. Even though I enjoy using a bread machine which has made only one bad loaf in its entire life—when the power went off before the baking cycle kicked in—I still don't think of bread when I think of life-giving food. In fact, I can go for weeks without eating a piece of bread. When I think of life-giving food I think of *sarma*, the heavenly national dish of Croatia. Sarma is somewhat similar to povatica, but better. In Chapter 7, I said that povatica was delivered from heaven by angels—sarma was delivered by archangels! It's better than povatica—it's made out of MEAT! "I myself am the sarma of life." Now that's more like it. What an improvement over "I myself am the bread of life." I hope you don't find my reconstructionism offensive or blasphemous. In truth, Jesus was using the best metaphor he could use for his time and place. In the Near East of Jesus, bread was the main life-giving food. Even today it is ubiquitous on the streets of Jerusalem— dipped into a variety of sauces, it easily becomes the main course. If Jesus were to return to Jerusalem now, he would probably use the bread metaphor again—but if he were to visit Croatia today, he would use sarma.

So in these final verses Jesus replaces "bread" with "flesh." "He who feeds on my flesh / and drinks my blood / has life eternal." The verb here is very realistic, more like "munch" or "gnaw," the kind of thing lions do with prey. I've always found it curious that Protestants, in the main, interpret these verses figuratively, It's curious because they generally interpret Scripture more literally than Catholics. It's also curious because of verse 60: "After hearing his words, many of his disciples remarked, 'This sort of talk is hard to endure!'"

"Just as . . . I have life because of the Father, / so the man who feeds on me will have life because of me." (Jn 6:57)—a striking way of saying: "You are what you eat." "If you do not eat the flesh of the Son of Man . . . / you have no life in you" (Jn 6:53). Given the power and clarity of these words, I'm perplexed that only 26% of Catholics attend mass regularly.

"For my flesh is real food / and my blood real drink" (Jn 6:55). Catholics believe in the "real" presence—at least we used to. Recent polls show that the percentage of Catholics who believe in the "real" presence is dropping. The eucharistic presence of Jesus is mysterious because it is not experienced; it is not a physical presence. Nevertheless, it is a real presence in that the eucharistic bread and wine actually become the substance of Christ's body and blood—this is why we genuflect when we come into the eucharistic presence of Christ.

Some years ago while I was in a rural sacristy somewhere in Wisconsin getting ready for Saturday night liturgy, I put unconsecrated altar breads in a ciborium. A few minutes later when I was ready to take them to the gift table, I couldn't find them. The sacristan, who also happened to be the director of religious education, was in the sacristy with me. She solved my quandary. After I asked: "Do you know what happened to the hosts?" she replied: "I put them in the tabernacle."

Twenty-some years ago I served as a chaplain at a summer camp we ran for inner-city boys and girls. Preaching to ten-year-old children can prove to be a daunting task.

However, on one of those summer Sundays I scored big with my homily. The gospel passage was John 6 and I based my sermon on the extraordinary events of the previous Thursday. Thursday was the regular cook's day off, so other staff cooked instead. Two of the male counselors signed up to cook breakfast on that Thursday and decided to make donuts. My, oh my! These donuts were something else. Hockey pucks with holes! Without the holes they actually would have weighed as much as hockey pucks. No one ate the things so, needless to say, there were a lot of them left over. Being a child of the Depression, and very frugal, I came up with a recycling idea. I would use them for my costume. We had a parade every Thursday afternoon. The camp staff dressed up in costume and marched in the parade one by one. The campers were the spectators and they selected the prize-winning costume. I won first prize that Thursday afternoon.

Time was of the essence, so I had to act fast. I gathered up the ninety-nine donuts and began to sew them, one by one, on my blue running suit. In the end I was covered from head to foot with them. The final touch was breathtaking. I took the final two donuts, connected them together, and made a pair of goggles! (Somewhere I have a picture.) When Mr. Donut appeared in the parade line, the unimaginable happened. *En masse,* the children ran toward me, attacked me, and started to eat me. What previously was inedible was now the "bread from heaven." I don't know how much life they took from me, but in that moment they had an unforgettable experience of John 6: 52–58. The sermon on Sunday consisted simply of recalling the memorable parade that happened on the previous Thursday.

14

Whenever Anyone Looked at the Bronze Serpent, He Recovered

In punishment the LORD sent among the people saraph serpents, which bit the people so that many of them died. Then the people came to Moses and said, "We have sinned in complaining against the LORD and you. Pray the LORD to take the serpents from us." So Moses prayed for the people, and the LORD said to Moses, "Make a saraph and mount it on a pole, and if anyone who has been bitten looks at it, he will recover." Moses accordingly made a bronze serpent and mounted it on a pole, and whenever anyone who had been bitten looked at the bronze serpent, he recovered. (Num 21:6–8)

Those forty years that lay between the Exodus and the entrance into the promised land were chuck full of complaining and murmuring in the desert of sin. As we read about this period in Exodus and Numbers, it seems that's all the people had time for—complaining and murmuring. Their behavior was obnoxious and annoying in the extreme, for they seem to have had absolutely no memory of the great deeds God did for them in delivering them from Egypt. Numbers 11 is a good illustration of the problem. The people tired of the manna and complained, "Would that we had meat for food! We remember the fish we used to eat without cost in Egypt, and the cucumbers"—and so on and so on. The Lord's response is comical. He tells Moses to announce to the people: "Therefore the LORD will give you meat for food, and you will eat it, not for one day, or two days, or five, or ten, or twenty days, but for a whole month—until it comes out of your very nostrils. . . ." How's that for an anthropomorphic passage of Scripture? Aggravating as they were, though, the Lord's love for his people triumphed in the end. In fact, the reason why Moses was denied entrance into the promised land was due his doubting of the Lord's compassion for his people. When the people complained about having no water to drink, the Lord commanded Moses to strike the rock with his staff. Before doing so he said, "Listen to me, you rebels! Are we to bring water for you out of this rock?" (Num 20:10) His sin here consisted in doubting God's mercy. God then told him, "Because you were not faithful to me in showing forth my sanctity before the Israelites, you shall not lead this community into the land I will give them" (Num 20:12).

The figure of the bronze serpent, described above in Numbers 21, speaks for itself. One of the first things we notice about the figure is that it illustrates that "God writes straight with crooked lines," and also the well-known aphorism, "being cured by the dog that bit you." Here, in a sense, God uses evil to fight evil. We, however, are forbidden the license to fight evil with evil. There is an even more dramatic illustration of God using evil to fight evil—the cross. "For our sakes God made him who did not know sin, to be sin, so that in him we might become the very holiness of God" (2 Cor 5:21).

Jesus applies the figure of the bronze serpent to himself in John 6:40. He does this quietly and, more or less, between the lines—in fact one would have to be familiar with Numbers 21 in order to know that Jesus was referring here to the bronze serpent: "Indeed, this is the will of my Father, that everyone who looks upon the Son and believes in him shall have eternal life." It's the "who looks upon" that makes this sentence a reference to Numbers 21. In other words, Jesus is saying: "I am the bronze serpent." This is a truly great figure because it's vivid, succinct, and ever so simple to get. I'm sure it was a favorite of Luther because it sums up his insight about justification without works. The "no work" aspect of the figure is absolutely perfect. Here we have people dying because of snakebite, and what do they have to do to be healed? Precious little. All they have to do is to look at the bronze serpent. How much energy does that take? Speaking as a physicist, I'd say about one erg's worth—believe me, that's not a lot. So there you have the whole doctrine of justification in a very simple analogy.

Chapter 3 of Romans is filled with the theology of justification by faith. A summation is made in 4:4: "Now, when a man works, his wages are not regarded as a favor but as his due. But when a man does nothing, yet believes in him who justifies the sinful, his faith is credited as justice." This is it! We are saved by the shear gratuitous mercy of God, not by anything we do. Biblical faith is not the same thing as what we normally think of when we think of faith. Faith for Catholics is generally an act of the will compelling the mind to assent to a revealed truth. The mind assents to the truth not because it is seen to be true or can be proved to be true, but simply because it is revealed by God. Acts of this kind proceed from the theological habit of faith. The faith of Romans 3 is not this but rather, the act of appropriating to oneself the forgiveness-giving and life-giving action of Jesus dying on the cross and being raised from the dead. This it the kind of faith that triggers justification.

In one of his sermons, St. Cyril of Jerusalem likened Jesus to a gladiator fighting an enemy who is an amalgam of the devil, sin, and death. Jesus is victorious over this enemy and stands over him with his sword drawn over his enemy's neck. We are spectators in the Colosseum. All we have to do is applaud. All we have to do is applaud, lightly, if you will—we don't want to expend a lot of energy because "no work" is the whole point of biblical salvific faith. We don't earn our being made right with God; we only have to accept it.

At the risk of working against the figure and muddying up what is perfectly clear, I feel compelled to be more circumspect and to say something about works. It's true that we're initially saved without doing anything except believing, i.e., putting our trust in the meritorious saving action of Jesus on the cross. But later on, works are required. Paul says, "For we hold that a man is justified by faith apart from observance of the law" (Rom 3:28). On the other hand, James says, "You must perceive that a person is justified by his works and not by faith alone" (Jas 2:24). It will come as no surprise to learn that Luther was not fond of the Epistle of James. In truth, both faith and works are required. Both Paul and James are true, they just approach the problem from different directions. Initial sanctifying grace comes through faith alone, but works must then follow. Otherwise faith will be proved to be an insincere faith.

Notwithstanding the previous paragraph, the figure of the bronze serpent is powerful, indeed. It should prove to be a valuable tool for prayer. The underlying reality of the figure is, once again, news too good to be believed. God saves us without anything required on our part: "It is precisely in this that God proves his love for us: that while we were still sinners, Christ died for us" (Rom 5:8). Sometimes we need simply to look upon the crucified Jesus and believe that he is God's bronze serpent, God's healing for snakebite and anything else that ails us.

15

Unless You Become Like Children

"What were you discussing on the way home?" At this they fell silent, for on the way they had been arguing about who was the most important. So he sat down and called the Twelve around him and said, "If anyone wishes to rank first, he must remain the last one of all and the servant of all." Then he took a little child, stood him in their midst, and putting his arms around him, said to them. "Whoever welcomes a child such as this for my sake welcomes me. And whoever welcomes me welcomes, not me, but him who sent me." (Mk 9:33–37)

This passage from Mark 9 is not to be confused with another of Jesus' encounters with children in Mark 10. In chapter 10, Jesus calls us to become like children insofar as children are docile believers. The encounter in chapter 9 is linked not to docility but to compassion and service: "If anyone wishes to be first, he shall be the last of all and the servant of all." Here Jesus is calling us to become like children insofar as children are lowly and powerless. Because we live two thousand years after the event, we're apt to miss the significance of Jesus' action in the above incident. In Jesus' time, children were not highly regarded and doted over—in fact, they were basically overlooked and ignored, as our culture overlooks and ignores the poor. They were, in fact, a despised lot. This being the case, Jesus, in befriending this child, in putting his arms around the child, was giving us a supreme example of what servanthood is all about. Jesus' action in our day and age would be like picking up a wet child! And who finds any degree of comfort in that? Only one who is already wet! Wetness provides the common bond that leads to the compassionate act of picking up a wet child.

Jesus is telling us that we must become poor and needy if we are to be of help to the poor and needy. Only those who are poor and needy and weak will be able to identify with those who are poor and needy and weak.

This action is similar in many respects to the humility Jesus displayed in washing the feet of the apostles. Foot-washing in Jesus' day was a work of humble service ordinarily performed by slaves. Here again we are at a disadvantage because of the two-thousand-year cultural gap. Our only experience of foot-washing occurs in a liturgical context. However, the foot-washing of Holy Thursday doesn't begin to do justice to the text because the "twelve apostles" always make sure that their feet are washed beforehand. This reminds me of a foot-washing I witnessed and will never forget, about twenty years ago—one of the twelve was wearing panty hose! Once, also about twenty years ago, I gave a pair of shoes to an indigent man at a Franciscan shelter on skid row in Chicago. He immediately put them on after hurriedly discarding the work shoes he had on, shoes he had not taken off for many weeks. That would have been the time for me to do some real foot-washing!

St. Paul sheds further light on this first/last paradox in 2 Cor 12:7–9: "In order that I might not become conceited I was given a thorn in the flesh, an angel of Satan to beat me and keep me from getting proud. Three times I begged the Lord that this might leave me. He said to me, 'My grace is enough for you, for in weakness power reaches perfection.' And so I willingly boast of my weaknesses instead, that the power of Christ may rest upon me." "In weakness power reaches perfection." What a sublime paradox to ponder! First we must face and accept our weaknesses, our flawedness, our sinfulness. Then, and only then, will we be empowered to be servants. Then, and only then, will we be compassionate. Similarity is the matrix of love; dissimilarity is the matrix of distrust and hate. St. Bernard puts it this way: *"Ex miseria discimus misericordiam."* ("It is from *misery* that we learn *mercy."*)

There's a powerful modern-day illustration of our own weaknesses leading to compassion—I'm thinking of Alcoholics Anonymous. "Hello, my name is Joe and I'm an alcoholic." There are no aliens in the AA meeting room (except, perhaps, for a few guests). All are perceived as other selves. The common bond is the weakness, the powerlessness, the sinfulness of alcoholism. And what a powerful bond it is; how that bond leads to mutual love and service within the body! I have friends in AA who would literally give their lives in service to their friends in AA. I know many sponsors in AA who take phone calls twenty-four hours a day from their charges and they do it gladly. Most in AA will say that they thank God for the gift of alcoholism: "And so I willingly boast of my weaknesses instead, that the power of Christ may rest upon me."

"Reform your lives, the kingdom of heaven is at hand" (Mt 4:17). It's interesting that both John the Baptist and Jesus began their preaching ministries with these same words. The call to repentance or reformation occurs over fifty times in the New Testament. The noun form in Greek is *metanoia,* which is a turning, a change of mind or heart as in the somewhat archaic: "I repent of ever having married you." It's a turning, but not necessarily a turning away from sin. It can mean a turning toward God in a new way. I like the way some Spanish Bibles translate the word: "taking a new road." I like this because, believe it or not, there are a great number of people who don't think that they need to turn away from sin. Thousands of them exist—I wish I had a dime for all those I ministered to in hospitals who told me on their deathbeds: "Father, I don't need to confess because I don't sin." It's far easier to get oneself or others to see the need for turning to God in a new way.

The parable of the Pharisee and the tax collector illustrates the need for repentance (Lk 18:9–14): "The Pharisee took up his position and spoke this prayer to himself, 'O God, I thank you that I am not like the rest of humanity—

greedy, dishonest, adulterous. . . .'" Notice that this trans-lation has him speaking to himself, not to God. His weak-ness lay precisely in his perceived strength of having it "all together." He was unable to repent. Pharisees fell under Jesus' condemnation, not primarily because they were hyp-ocrites but because they were full of themselves, spiritually self-satisfied and incapable of repentance.

This parable is not as easy as it first appears. For exam-ple, with whom should we identify? Most make the wrong choice and identify with the tax collector. "O God, be mer-ciful to me a sinner." But if we go this route, then we're already there, without the need to repent, the need to take another road. No, when we read this parable we should identify with the Pharisee. Reflection on his attitude will then bring us to beg God for honesty: "O God, I thank you that I am like the rest of humanity." One of the problems with the Pharisee's list is that it is too short. He may not have been an adulterer, but a longer list would have made him stop in his tracks—would have made him realize that he too was in need of repentance.

"Those who are healthy do not need a physician, but the sick do. I have not come to call the righteous to repen-tance but sinners" (Lk 5:31–32). These words of Jesus need some explication. The key word here is *repentence*. He has come for the righteous too, not *qua* righteous but *qua* sick. It's too facile to divide the world into sinners and saints—in fact, what makes a saint a saint is a radical self-aware-ness of neediness. The world is comprised of sinners and repentant sinners. Realizing that repentance is an ongoing process, each of us is in continual need of it.

This power/weakness paradox, however, is not as enigmatic as it first seems when we consider that our real power to be holy and to be true disciples of Jesus comes from grace, which is usually the result of prayer. Weakness brings us to our knees, whereas power keeps us upright and isolated from God and ultimately from others and their needs. The power/weakness paradox is really the same as the rich/poor paradox of the Gospels. Riches make one poor spiritually because they give a false sense of secu-rity and isolate one from God and the needs of others.

"Blessed are the poor in spirit." Blessed are those who are down and out, for they are the ones who will pray to God for help; they are the ones who will identify with others in their need. They are the ones who will pick up the wet children of the world.

16

From Now on You Will Be Catching Men

"Put out into the deep water and lower your nets for a catch." Simon answered, "Master, we have been hard at it all night long and have caught nothing; but if you say so, I will lower the nets." Upon doing this they caught such a great number of fish that their nets were at the breaking point. They signaled to their mates in the other boat to come and help them. These came, and together they filled the two boats until they nearly sank . . . amazement at the catch they had made seized [Peter] and all his shipmates, as well as James and John. . . . Jesus said to Simon, "Do not be afraid. From now on you will be catching men." With that they brought their boats to land, left everything, and became his followers. (Lk 5:4–11)

In this passage Jesus uses the prosaic figure of fishing to great effect. The meaning is clear: The apostles are to evangelize and God will greatly bless their labors. As with every analogy, this one limps a bit—fish are killed after they are caught! The evangelical reality is just the opposite, and we see it illustrated in that catch of the first two fish, James and John; in being caught, they are given life in abundance. This gospel vignette is very succinct, nonetheless; it implies a Jesus who is utterly charismatic and attractive—so attractive, in fact, that a brief encounter with him causes one to abandon all and follow him.

Evangelism has never been a popular word with Catholics. In fact, just hearing the word is likely to produce tremors of fear. For many Catholics, the word bespeaks the freaky intrusive behavior of those who knock on one's door and attempt to play recordings. Jehovah's Witnesses, God bless them, put Christians to shame when it comes to proselytizing zeal. When I was a chaplain at St. Mary's Hospital in Madison, Wisconsin, Jehovah's Witness patients were always trying to evangelize me. I would retaliate by evangelizing them—pointing out to them that there is no "Jehovah," that they should be called "Yahweh's Witnesses." (The word *Jehovah* is a mistranslation occurring in many English Bibles. *Yahweh* is God's name as revealed by him to Moses in Exodus 3:14. However, the name was too sacred to pronounce, so in its place *Adonai* [Lord] was read. The later seventh-century addition of the vowel points of "Adonai" to the consonants YHWH in the Hebrew texts produced the hybrid "Jehovah.") Alas, my efforts were of no avail.

Vatican II, however, had a lot to say about evangelism. In fact, its teaching on evangelism is arguably one of its two most important teachings—the other being its teaching that there is no second-class membership in the Church, that each and every member of the Church is called to holiness. The clear teaching of the council on evangelism is similar: the Church by its very nature is evangelistic, and each and every member of the Church is called to the task of evangelism. How different these teachings are from what I grew up with fifty years ago. If one wanted to be holy, one became a priest or religious. If one wanted to evangelize, one became a priest or religious. This is not to say that the new teaching of Vatican II has taken root in Catholics. The new teaching is thirty-five years old and it will take at least that much more time for it to be a part of our ordinary thinking.

The need for evangelization is perhaps greater today than it has ever been. While it is true that the faith grew very rapidly in the first centuries of the Christian era, there has been little or no growth in the present century. Africa is a striking exception, a Christian population of ten million at the beginning of the century has grown to one hundred million. It is sad to contemplate that after twenty centuries only 20% of the present world population is Christian. Atheism, materialistic evolution, materialism, and a general mistrust of organizations all contribute to the present need to evangelize. Even though the United States is considered relatively religious among Western nations, recent polls show that in excess of eighty million adults in the United States can be classified as unchurched. This means that while you wait in line at the checkout counter there is about a 100% chance that either the person in front of you or the person behind you is in need of evangelization, in need of hearing the good news of the gospel. (I'm assuming that you're not waiting in line with your spouse.)

As I say this I can almost feel your fear that I'm going to suggest that you speak to that unchurched person about Jesus while you're waiting in line. Fear not, for that would be freaky. Notice how nonthreatening and natural is the evangelization of Jesus described in the above gospel passage. It takes place in the context of fishing and comes out of Jesus' desire to share life with others. James and John experience goodness, human and divine, in Jesus and cannot but leave all and follow him. This experience of Jesus, and the many that will follow, will provide them with the wherewithal to continue the work of evangelization. The condition *sine qua non* of evangelization is experience. The need for experience cannot be over emphasized. One cannot share the good news (read Jesus) if one has not first heard and experienced the good news. Since the task of evangelization is incumbent upon every Christian, the Spirit of Jesus will certainly reveal Jesus to every disciple who asks for the grace of experiencing Jesus. This was the grace conferred at Pentecost, and there's every reason to believe that the same grace is available today.

An analogy is in order. I have a special love for water which began in my college years when I spent my summers as a lifeguard at my hometown's municipal swimming pool. These summers were the happiest of my life. They were filled with a lot of hard twelve-hour work days but, more importantly, they were filled with many good times with friends—my whole gang worked at the pool. It pains me now to go back to Creston. The pool has been torn down. Come to think of it, so has the roundhouse, my parish school, my parish church, and my high school. Either I'm getting old or there is a conspiracy afoot to obliterate all traces of my ever having lived there.

Since those halcyon summers I've almost drowned twice, but have managed to maintain my love for water. It's interesting how a former lifeguard faces drowning—always with a great deal of disbelief. In the five years following my ordination I used to sail the waters of Cape Cod for two weeks every summer with five other Dominicans on a thirty-eight foot ketch—now those truly were the good old days. Over the past ten years I've "worked" from time to time as a chaplain on cruise ships, mostly in the Caribbean—it's hard and dirty work, but someone has to do it!

The gospel passage quoted above mentions boats, so my mind naturally turns to my boating experience. I preface the following cruise ship figure with a plea to overlook my overlooking of the dangers associated with soaking up the sun's rays. I can compare the world and its need to be evangelized to the passengers of a cruise ship. Many of the passengers on a cruise ship live a substandard life because of their ignorance of the upper deck. They spend far too much time in their cabins, some of which are below the water line or without portholes. Some passengers spend too much of their time in the casino trying to make an elusive jackpot amid all the smoke. These passengers are poor (perhaps an oxymoron since only 8% of Americans can afford to cruise) because they know nothing of the upper deck. God bless the upper deck! This is where it's at. This is where there's life in abundance. This is where there's real living. There are swimming pools up there and the sun almost always shines. The glorious sun! There's nothing comparable to spending time under a Caribbean sun on the upper deck at poolside. It's not uncomfortably hot, as the ship produces about fifteen knots of cooling breeze by simply moving through the water. There are good things to drink on the upper deck, like frosted margaritas, and great things to eat, like blackened chicken. There are also pool-of-Bethesda-like whirlpools on the upper deck which provide healing from all sorts of physical aches and pains.

After experiencing the good life in the sun on the upper deck, it's the most natural thing in the world to tell others about it—notice how natural and non-freaky it is for me to tell you about the upper deck. Telling others becomes one's major goal for the time left on board. Most of those below are not on the upper deck simply because no one ever told them how good life is up there.

In many ways this describes the Christian life. One of its major tasks is to get more and more people into the sun (read Son). One doesn't need to knock on cabin doors to tell the good news; it can be conveyed very naturally and sincerely, e.g., over lunch on days when there's open seating in the dining room. For most of the passengers a word to the wise is sufficient; once they experience for themselves the fullness of life on the upper deck, they themselves will become evangelists. Others are perhaps crippled and will need help in getting to the upper deck. No matter; one who has experienced the upper deck will be more than happy to help others get there.

One final word of caution. When bringing passengers to the upper deck, make sure that they are distributed evenly on the port and starboard. We don't want a repeat of the Chicago River *Eastland* tragedy. I just remembered, I forgot to tell you that the ship's one port of call is Dubrovnik, arguably the most beautiful city in the world. (Dubrovnik, a Croation ciy on the Dalmatian coast, is not far from the island of Kortula, the birthplace of Marco Polo; he, too, was Croatian.) This is the city of St. Blaise (St. Vlaha), who was bishop there in the third century. There is a church in his honor on the main street of this carless walled paradise; the street is made of polished white stone and is literally clean enough to eat on. The city reminds one of Revelation 21: "The city had the radiance of a precious jewel that sparkled like a diamond. . . . The foundation of the city wall was ornate with precious stones of every sort."

Dubrovnik is a "must see" city—both literally and figuratively.

17

Moved With Pity, the Master Wrote Off the Debt

The reign of God may be said to be like a king who decided to settle accounts with his officials. When he began his auditing, one was brought in who owed him a huge amount. As he had no way of paying it, his master ordered him to be sold, along with his wife, his children, and all his property, in payment of the debt. At that the official prostrated himself in homage and said, "My lord, be patient with me and I will pay you back in full." Moved with pity, the master let the official go and wrote off the debt. But when that same official went out he met a fellow servant who owed him a mere fraction of what he himself owed. He seized him and throttled him. "Pay back what you owe," he demanded. His fellow servant dropped to his knees and began to plead with him, "Just give me time and I will pay you back in full." But he would hear none of it. Instead, he had him put in jail until he paid back what he owed. When his fellow servants saw what had happened they were badly shaken, and went to their master to report the whole incident. His master sent for him and said. "You worthless wretch!" (Mt 18:23–32)

The above parable speaks for itself. Nevertheless, as always, I have a few thoughts about it. First I want to

quote a news story which appeared in the *Chicago Tribune*—
I kid you not.

> *A judge put a lock on an 84-year-old woman's tele-*
> *phone and threatened to return her to a penal farm*
> *in hopes of forcing her to stop harassing a man she*
> *has telephoned 10 times a day ever since he reported*
> *her dog to the Humane Society—in 1937.*
>
> *But A. Douglas Thompson, who was delivering*
> *newspapers when Gertrude Jamison's shaggy white*
> *dog leaped from the bushes and nipped him that*
> *afternoon, thinks it will take more than that to stop*
> *the calls that have been a part of his life for 45 years.*
> *For business reasons he never sought an unlisted*
> *number, he said.*
>
> *"She'll call again, I guarantee you," Thompson*
> *said after a court hearing Thursday for his tormen-*
> *tor. "As long as she can dial a phone, she'll call."*
>
> *However, Frank Groves, the prosecuting attor-*
> *ney, thinks Jamison's age is catching up with her.*
>
> *"If she were able to get around, I'd agree with*
> *Mr. Thompson," Groves said. "I think she would go*
> *out and make more calls. But I think we've got a*
> *good chance to stop it now, mainly because she's in*
> *poor health and not as active as she used to be."*
>
> *Jamison has been charged about a dozen times*
> *with making the annoying calls over the years, pros-*
> *ecutors said.*
>
> *Jamison, who was sent to the workhouse—a*
> *penal farm—in 1965 when she refused to promise a*
> *judge she would stop the calls, made that pledge to*
> *Criminal Court Judge Russell Hinson after he raised*
> *the specter of another term.*
>
> *Thompson was 16 when he was nipped on the*
> *heel and reported the dog to the Humane Society,*
> *which kept the pet under observation for a few days*
> *before returning it.*
>
> *"She got a little upset over that," Thompson said.*

This second story also speaks for itself. It's funnier than
the parable, but I also find the parable humorous—the

unforgiving servant's behavior is outrageous to the point of being ludicrous. It's great to have a little humor around when we examine that saddest of human faults, unforgiveness. Seeing humor in the unforgiveness of others at least gives us a peek at the phenomenon and opens up the possibility of examining the same traits in ourselves. My favorite ecclesiastical story on unforgiveness is the following true story related to me by Cornelius Hahn, O.P.:

> *Three times Pius X named Giacomo della Chiesa, archbishop of Bologna, a cardinal. Three times Cardinal Merry del Val vetoed the nomination—he was secretary of state. The third time Pius X wrote it back in. That was May 1914. In August 1914 Pius X died—and della Chiesa was elected Benedict XV. At the obedience, when Merry del Val knelt before him, Benedict XV said: "We forgive Caro—but we don't forget."*

I think a good part of our difficulty in dealing with unforgiveness is a result of confusion. We confuse the emotional part of unforgiveness with the sinful part. Since the two are linked together in our thinking, and since we know that we can't control the emotional part, we get frightened and look the other way. Even though Scripture shows an angry Jesus from time to time, one would have to say that, in general, the Bible seems to come down hard on the so called negative emotions. For example, we have passages like the following: "Anyone who hates his brother is a murderer" (1 Jn 3:15). However, it's important to note that most of the time the Bible does not distinguish between feeling an emotion and expressing an emotion. It's never a sin to have or feel an emotion—even the negative emotions such as anger or hatred. Having emotions can't be sinful because we do not have willful control over our emotions. There's a difference between feeling an emotion and expressing an emotion—and sometimes it's objectively sinful to express an emotion. To illustrate this I have another quotation from a news article from the *Chicago Tribune*:

> *A Catholic priest has been charged with assault after an artistic disagreement with a tambourine player in which he allegedly threw her down the stairs and slugged the church youth director. Rev. Thomas Woerth of St. Joseph's Catholic Church is accused of pushing Mary Ellen Watterson, 18, after a church service. Watterson said "Father Woerth had a problem with the way I play the tambourine."*

A distinction also needs to be made between the emotional and the spiritual. To hate another emotionally is not a sin and, in no way, implies spiritual hatred, which is a sin. Let's say you're out in a boat with someone you emotionally hate. She falls overboard. What do you do then? Extend the oar to her to help her get back on board—or hit her with the oar? You answer, "I'd help her, certainly." This response proves that you love your enemy, you love her spiritually. The sin of hatred, on the other hand, includes the desire that evil might fall on one's enemy.

And who is my enemy? An enemy is a person who has hurt me, either intentionally or unintentionally, or a person who has disappointed me in some way. It's amazing how many people hurt us without meaning to—if only there were some easy way to bring their behavior to their attention without, in some cases, making the problem worse. What is forgiveness? Since we can't control our negative emotions, forgiveness, at least in its early stages, doesn't require much on our part. It consists mainly in a decision to be willing to let go of the hurt and let it heal. It doesn't require a decision to be friends again—this, after all, is impossible if the emotions of anger or hatred are still present. But it does require an openness to the possibility of friendship sometime in the future. All this doesn't sound like a lot, but it is a lot—if a lot of anger or hatred is present.

Generosity goes a long way in forgiveness. The more we have of it, the more forgiving we'll be. The incident of the penitent woman and Jesus' parable in Luke 7 helps us a great deal in this regard:

> *"Two men owed money to a certain money-lender;*
> *one owed a total of five hundred coins, the other*
> *fifty. Since neither was able to repay, he wrote off*
> *both debts. Which of them was more grateful to*
> *him?" Simon answered, "He, I presume, to whom he*
> *remitted the larger sum." Jesus said to him, "You*
> *are right."*
>   *Turning then to the woman, he said to Simon:*
> *"You see this woman? I came to your home and you*
> *provided me with no water for my feet. She has*
> *washed my feet with her tears and wiped them with*
> *her hair. . . . I tell you that is why her many sins are*
> *forgiven—because of her great love. Little is forgiven*
> *the one whose love is small."*

Until recently, this was the lectionary version and it has an egregious translation error. The new translation gets it right: "So I tell you, her many sins have been forgiven; hence, she has shown great love." In other words, her loving compassionate behavior is not a cause of her forgiveness but a cause of Jesus' knowledge of that forgiveness. The older lectionary translation puts the theological cart ahead of the horse, and it directly contradicts the meaning of the underlying parable.

The last sentence of the corrupt translation is equally heretical: "Little is forgiven the one whose love is small." In the new translation, the last sentence is translated correctly. It is of equal importance: "But the one to whom little is forgiven, loves little." This is not a mandate to go out and sin boldly. Rather, it tells us that we will be generous, compassionate, and loving to the extent that we realize how much we have been forgiven. Notice how this principle is at work in the lives of the saints. They annoy us in their writings with constant declarations of their sinfulness—yet this awareness is the foundation of their heroic charity and compassion.

I have one more practical idea to add to these recipes for forgiveness. Father Joseph Lang in one of his books talks about a relational problem he had with a pastor while he was an associate pastor—for a whole litany of reasons, he

hated him. Then the pastor suddenly ended up in a hospital, seriously ill. Joseph went to see him and suddenly saw
him with new eyes. His vision was transfigured and, for the
first time, he saw the pastor not as vicious but as sick. This
was indeed a moment of grace, for from then on their relationship changed; they eventually became friends. You
might want to try this strategy on your enemies, but don't
let them know—your erstwhile enemies will not be amused
and might even come back to life if they find out that you
regard them as sick.

18

Take My Yoke Upon Your Shoulders

Come to me, all you who are weary and find life burdensome, and I will refresh you. Take my yoke upon your shoulders and learn from me, for I am gentle and humble of heart. Your souls will find rest, for my yoke is easy and my burden is light. (Mt 11:28–30)

In this passage Jesus uses two figures, "burden" and "yoke." They are quite distinct, but likely to be confused. In the context both are paradoxical, especially Jesus' use of "burden." You'll need the help of the Holy Spirit to wrap your mind around the idea that Jesus' burden, light as it is, is better than no burden at all. Conventional wisdom dictates otherwise. When we think of Jesus' burden *vis-à-vis* the burden of the Pharisees, we instinctively judge Jesus' to be lighter. After all, Jesus' interpretation of God's law was shorter and more to the point than that of the Pharisees. But what about Matthew 5:20? "I tell you, unless your holiness surpasses that of the scribes and Pharisees you shall not enter the kingdom of God." A good case can be made that Jesus places a heavier burden on his disciples than did the Pharisees on theirs. Jesus demands internal as well as external compliance with God's law of love and justice: "You Pharisees! You cleanse the outside of cup and dish but within you are filled with rapaciousness and evil" (Lk 11:39).

Once an enthusiastic disciple approached Jesus and said; "Teacher, I will follow you wherever you go" (Mt 8:19). Jesus said to him: "The foxes have holes, and birds of the air have nests; but the Son of Man has nowhere to lay his head" (Mt 8:20). As a comic aside, someone once told me that there is a church somewhere in Europe that has the rock on which Jesus "had not" to lay his head. More seriously, Jesus' reply should elicit from us not "Poor Jesus" but "Poor me." In Luke 14 Jesus presents two parables that describe the great difficulty inherent in being one of his disciples. In one he compares discipleship to building a great tower; in the other he compares discipleship to launching a military campaign against one's enemy. In other words, one needs to consider the cost before enlisting: Wimps need not apply. The Lord, like the Marines, is looking for a few good men and women.

This being the case, how does one explain the current statistic that only 26% of Catholics in the U.S. attend mass regularly? Why are we so undisciplined when it comes to discipleship? I'm reminded of my Catholic grammar-school experience. Some subjects were taught religiously, namely religion and the three Rs. Whenever we needed to make some extra time in the schedule, we went for the second-class subjects, i.e., we skipped geography and music. I didn't mention gym class because we didn't have gym class. Discipleship is regarded in the same way, as unimportant, and as second class—sleep on Sunday morning is more important than mass. Wait a minute, what am I thinking? One can attend mass now on Saturday. When I was a hospital chaplain, patients would tell me that they didn't go to mass. "The reason is not neglect, Father, but a job that forces me to work on Sunday." Then I would jump in with: "But you can now go on Saturday." Next I would find myself looking at a face filled with amazement and incredulity.

Before turning from the figure of "burden" to the other, easier figure of "yoke," I'd like to say that I'm somewhat of an expert on burdens. I grew up in southwest Iowa and remember suffering through those Iowa summers. I even remember a summer when we had over thirty consecutive days with temperatures over one hundred degrees. I also need to point out that these were the days before houses or cars had air-conditioning. This fact alone explains why so many went to the movies in those days. And where was I during those dog days of summer? I was practicing football in full uniform, twice a day, for two hours at a time. Talk about burdens! "We know that affliction makes for endurance, and endurance for tested virtue. . . ." (Rom 5:3–4). Those burdensome days were some of the most important of my life as they produced within me an above-average degree of the virtue of long-suffering.

I played football only because I was influenced by an older friend, Jim, who loved the game and convinced me that going out for football would improve my image—classical pianists are always in need of image adjustments. In other words, I was driven solely by human respect. However, this single experience inured me, in a remarkable way, to other hardships I would later face—it truly made me strong, so I have no regrets. I wish I could say that my soul found rest in that football burden—but it didn't. Jim and I lived for the end of practice, after which we would go to Hanson's Drugstore for a freshly squeezed orangeade.

The other figure, "yoke," is much easier to understand. A yoke is a crossbar with two U-shaped pieces that encircle the necks of a pair of oxen or other draft animals working together. Notice that two animals are involved. In the yoke of discipleship we are yoked to Jesus. A yoke keeps us on the right path, on the "straight and narrow." A yoke limits freedom but, paradoxically, that's not necessarily a bad thing. St. Paul constantly enjoins us to become slaves of God so that we might be truly free and have eternal life (Rom 6:22).

Practically speaking, a yoke provides discipline. When we say that someone has discipline, we may be referring generically to a habit, a quality of soul like the moral virtues of prudence, temperance, justice, or fortitude. Or we may simply be saying that someone is under a yoke. In either case the results are the same: The person stays on the "straight and narrow."

I was a disciplined child, not in the sense that I had virtue but in the sense that I was under a yoke. My yoke was my mother. Because I was yoked to her, I practiced the piano for at least an hour a day. If I didn't, she would get me out of bed and send me to the piano. It was as simple as that. If I didn't practice, no matter what time of night it was, she would drag me down to the piano to practice. The mere threat of this was so powerful that I always practiced an hour a day. I was yoked. To go in another direction would have been too painful—and not worth it.

If we are to be true disciples of Jesus we need discipline. We need either the virtue of discipline or we need the discipline that comes from simply being yoked. It's amazing how undisciplined most of us are when it comes to fulfilling the requirements of discipleship. It's all the more amazing when we consider the arduousness of discipleship. How lightly we take those discipleship parables of Jesus.

We all know that our spiritual health depends on individual prayer time each day, yet how few of us are faithful to that practice. Why is it we can go for days without praying when we wouldn't think of going for days without flossing our teeth? Let me rephrase that: Why is it that we can go for days without praying when we wouldn't think of going for days without brushing our teeth? We lack discipline! We need a yoke. Most of us, as adults, don't have the luxury of having someone like my mother around to be that yoke. Therefore we have to provide that yoke ourselves. We need a self-imposed yoke to link us to Christ. It goes without saying that the honor system will be of paramount importance.

When someone comes to me for counseling and laments about not praying regularly, I talk discipline. "Decide what the punishment will be if you don't pray, say ten minutes, today. Let's say that you decide that you won't watch your favorite soap if you didn't pray for ten minutes the previous day. It's as simple as that; perhaps you'll never watch that program again. Let's say that you don't like TV. That's all right. Why not send me a quarter if you don't pray for ten minutes? What if, at the end of the week, you discover that you've sent me $1.75? What do you do then?" This actually was the case with one of my clients. I asked her: "So what do you do now?" She said: "I'll send you a nickel." I retorted: "Get real, you'll send me 50¢!" Sometimes it takes some fine-tuning to get the punishment to match the crime, but finally there will be a match and the crime will cease to exist. Why? Because it's simply not worth it.

A case can be made for, "You can be as holy as you want to be." When I first heard these words in a sermon almost fifty years ago, I thought the priest was exaggerating. But he backed up his statement with: "It is God's will that you grow in holiness" (1 Thes 4:3). If my holiness is God's will, then the wherewithal is also in God's will and waits only for my cooperation. Now, fifty years later, I tend to agree with that priest. At one poignant point in *What's Eating Gilbert Grape?*, Gilbert's six-hundred-pound mother says: "I never wanted to be this way." Perhaps she was exaggerating.

19

God's Eternal Power Has Become Visible, Recognized Through the Things He Has Made

The wrath of God is being revealed from heaven against the irreligious and perverse spirit of men who, in this perversity of theirs, hinder the truth. In fact, whatever can be known about God is clear to them; he himself made it so. Since the creation of the world, invisible realities, God's eternal power and divinity have become visible, recognized through the things he has made. Therefore these men are inexcusable. They certainly had knowledge of God, yet they did not glorify him as God or give him thanks. . . . In consequence, God delivered them up in their lust to unclean practices. (Rom 1: 18–24)

Next to Jesus himself, the created universe, in my opinion, is the most powerful icon of God. It pains me to make this assertion because very few would agree. What pains me is not the disagreement *per se*, but the underlying reason for it—what I would call pathological global blindness. What has happened in the last three hundred years in natural science and philosophy has produced a spiritual and intellectual blindness that is far more debilitating than total physical blindness. The effect of this blindness is that we are no longer able to see God in his creation.

We are far worse off than the pagans Paul describes in the above passage from Romans. They chose to be ignorant of the creator; we, on the other hand, are almost compelled to be ignorant of him, given the all-pervading materialistic evolutionism of the last one hundred fifty years. Material-istic evolutionism has deprived humankind of its most connatural joy: the joy of being able to glorify God in the reflected glory of the things that he has made. Twice in Ephesians 1 the author reminds us of our final cause: To be a people God has made his own, to praise his glory. Mate-rialistic evolutionism is one bad idea in the history of human thought that has done more harm than all other bad ideas combined. Its argument—that the scientific and intel-lectual world has swallowed wholesale—goes something like this: In the beginning there was hydrogen made up of nondescript bbs which we call protons or atoms. The forces acting on these bbs have a remarkable mathematical uni-formity and were described by Newton and his successors in the eighteenth and nineteenth centuries. Now, if you leave these bbs alone for a very long time and let them interact in a random way, you end up with the created uni-verse as we know it, including human beings. At first, you may think that this scenario is short on causality, and that I can't be serious. But you're not throwing in enough time—billions of years is what makes the difference.

Several years ago, when my father's aging fingers started to have difficulty in winding his magnificent 1938 Gruen Curvex watch, he decided to give the beauty to me—I never told him, but I too found it hard to wind. The next day I replaced the smallish stem. I'm looking at the mechanical marvel now—Swiss craftsmanship at its finest! Wait a minute! Did I say craftsmanship? Pardon me; there was no watchmaker. The watch never had a maker. It's just a cunning array of very tiny bbs that came together to form a watch. Impossible you say? You're not giving the process enough time.

My response to this is: Anyone who believes this will believe anything. Try building a 400 Mhz computer using this methodology. I'm using a 400 Mhz computer to write this book and I have a hard time believing that human beings could be smart enough to come up with it. And then I reflect on the fact that the human brain is almost infinitely more complicated than my computer. And to think that we didn't need a creator—that's almost too much to believe.

You're right! To deny materialistic evolutionism is not necessarily to deny evolution. Pope John Paul II, in fact, has recently supported the idea of evolution. I have not studied the question enough to come to a reasoned conclusion. Some evolution has occurred, certainly. The question: "How much?" is moot. At this time I'm not ready to admit of protozoan ancestors, but even if I did, this would not imply that God was not needed in the evolutionary process.

When I was attending Iowa State University, I remember driving to Chicago in the fall of 1954 with one of my physics professors and two other physics majors—we were going to visit Argonne National Laboratory on a senior field trip. The professor confided in us that he found the universe to be unbelievably beautiful and interconnected, unbelievably complicated and wonderful. In fact, he believed the universe was so marvelous that no one could be smart enough and powerful enough to design and create it—therefore he chose to be atheist. So much for common sense! I will give him this much: At least he didn't buy the bb argument.

An article appeared in the *New York Times* recently about the common housefly. The author was completely bowled over by the fly, which he considered to be an engineering marvel nonpareil. He went on for two pages, especially impressed with the aerodynamic prowess of flies and their ability to escape from most forms of human aggression. The article generally expressed my own thoughts about our universe and all that populates it. After reading it I almost vowed never to kill another fly. The author pointed out that the profligacy of nature is one of the reasons we so little appreciate these trillion-dollar engineering marvels. Perhaps if there were only one thousand flies, and they were on the endangered species list, they would be better appreciated. It's the same way with mosquitoes and corn. Driving through Iowa yesterday, I couldn't believe how many ears there were in those fields.

St. Thomas had no trouble coming up with five proofs for the existence of God. His proof from motion is somewhat flawed because he was relying on a flawed pre-Newtonian physics, but the other proofs continue to stand. His argument from design is the implied argument of Romans 1. It's interesting that Romans 1 was definitively interpreted by Vatican I and used to back up its solemn declaration that the existence of God can be proved from the existence of the created universe.

To say that materialistic atheistic evolutionism is the most pernicious idea in human intellectual history is corroborated by Romans 1: "The wrath of God is being revealed from heaven against the irreligious and perverse spirit of men. . . ." The word "irreligious" is sometimes translated as "impious," sometimes as "wicked." The word in Greek is *asebia*. *Asebia* is the antonym of *eusebia*, i.e., "piety." It is interesting that "impious" in English primarily means "wicked," rather than "not pious." The Roman martyrology constantly refers to the wicked emperors as impious. This is exactly the meaning that Paul gives it in Romans 1. *Asebia* is quintessential wickedness for Paul. Failure to give God thanks and to glorify him for the created universe is the "sin of sins." It is the capital sin, the sin that spawns all other sin. Romans 1:25–32 contains that non-exhaustive list of all the sins that follow in the wake of impiety, i.e., not thanking God.

A correlative argument can be made that if *asebia* is the father of all other sins, *eusebia* is the mother of all other virtues. In other words, if one has this one virtue—the virtue of being able to recognize God in his creation and being able to glorify him and thank him for this creation—then all the other virtues will come in due time. I can't pass up the opportunity to comment on 1 Timothy 3:16: "Wonderful, indeed is the mystery of our faith." This verse translates *"tes eusebiae mysterion,"* and is poorly translated in this lectionary version. This mistranslated phrase is also used by the priest at mass to elicit the memorial acclamation after the consecration: "Let us proclaim the mystery of faith." Since this verse introduces a Christological hymn in 1 Timothy, it definitely refers to Christ: "Wonderful, indeed, is (Jesus) that mystery of piety!" Jesus was the pious one. It's too bad that this adjective in English has taken on a pejorative meaning. Piety was Jesus' hallmark virtue. He was, and is, forever giving thanks to God for and on behalf of all creation. It's instructive to read "Wonderful, indeed, is (Jesus) that mystery of piety" and then read, say, the Gospel of Luke—on every page Jesus is giving thanks.

We desperately need to recapture our lost ability to see God in nature and to thank him for it. This is somewhat peripheral, but I think the reason it's harder and harder for Christians to believe in resurrection from the dead lies in the fact that we find it hard to believe that our present bodies were created by God. If we believed that our present bodies came from God, it wouldn't be so hard to believe that he could reconstruct them. But, more to the point, we need to recapture this virtue so that we will be more like Jesus, "that mystery of piety," "that mystery of thankfulness."

20

And There Are Eunuchs Who Have Made Themselves Eunuchs

His disciples said to him, "If such is the case of a man with his wife, it is better not to marry." But he said to them, "Not everyone can accept this teaching but only those to whom it is given. For there are eunuchs who have been so from birth, and there are eunuchs who have been made eunuchs by others, and there are eunuchs who have made themselves eunuchs for the sake of the kingdom of heaven. Let anyone accept this who can."
(Mt 19:10–12 NSRV)

Perhaps the funniest experience of my life occurred in the late sixties. I was the celebrant of a Sunday morning mass at a suburban parish in the Chicago area (I dare not say which one) shortly after the restoration of the permanent deaconate. One of the newly ordained permanent deacons of the archdiocese was the gospel reader for this mass. When he came to the word "eunuchs," he pronounced it "unches" (pronounced like inches). I came very close to "losing it." I think the funniest part of this gaffe lies in the fact that he repeated the word three times! Imagine trying to pull yourself together after this to deliver a homily!

"Eunuchs for the sake of the kingdom of heaven." What does this mean? There is a similar passage in Mark where Jesus says: "I give you my word, there is no one who has given up home, brothers or sisters, mother or father, children or property, for me and for the gospel who will not receive in this present age a hundred times as many homes. . . ." (Mk 10:29–30). "For me and for the gospel" is equivalent to "for the sake of the kingdom of heaven." It's interesting that wives aren't mentioned in the Markan passage. Celibacy, though, is implied in the giving up of home and children. These teachings of Jesus, no doubt, along with Jesus' own practice of celibacy and his teaching on asceticism, laid the foundation for what was to become the practice of Christian celibacy. But the "why" of religious celibacy is another question.

"For the sake of the gospel," for the most part, has been interpreted in the vein of time. If one gives up worldly cares and concerns, then there will be more time for the things of God, for the gospel. This is certainly the argument in 1 Corinthians: "An unmarried man is anxious about the things of the Lord, how he may please the Lord. But a married man is anxious about the things of the world, how he may please his wife, and he is divided" (1 Cor 7:32–33). Many would argue that this is the basic reason why celibacy has been mandatory for priests of the Western Catholic Church since the twelfth century. Certainly there is truth here. My own view, however, is that economics is the biggest albeit subconscious reason for extant clerical celibacy—it's much easier for a parish to support a priest than to support a priest and his wife and children. My own experience of clerical acquaintances, who are not Roman Catholic and who are married, militates against the "time for God" explanation of celibacy. All of these friends seem to have enough time for marriage and for the needs of the gospel. The outstanding example here would be the Rev. Martin E. Marty, who has authored more than five hundred books and articles.

By this time you're probably wondering how celibacy fits into a book on images of God. The answer is to be found in Luke 20. In answer to the hypothetical question posed him concerning the hapless widow with seven dead husbands, Jesus answered: "The children of this age marry and remarry; but those who are deemed worthy to attain to the coming age and to the resurrection of the dead neither marry nor are given in marriage. They can no longer die, for they are like angels; and they are the children of God because they are the ones who will rise" (Lk 20:34–6). These words of Jesus arguably provide the greatest rationale for religious celibacy: prophecy. Religious celibacy is primarily a prophetic action. It points to and bespeaks the time of the "new age," the time of the "new heavens and the new earth," a time in which there will not be marriage. At that time everyone will be celibate. An aside is in order here. All the theologians I've read are unanimous in asserting that there is no food or sex in heaven because of immortality. Immortality precludes the need for either sex or food. Several decades ago this was the topic of conversation at dinner in one of our priories. I'll never forget the crestfallen look on the face of one of the younger friars at the table— apparently this was something he had never heard before! This certainly gave him food for thought. I couldn't help but think of the *pro forma* words a prior asks a Dominican before accepting his solemn vows: "Knowing what you now know, do you want to go on?" In reaction to the "no food or sex in heaven" dictum, I've heard some strong reactions from lay people over the years, even, "Then why try to go there?" St. Paul says, "The world as we know it is passing away" (1 Cor 7:31). We have to believe that the goods of heaven include, in a transcendent way, all the goods of this world, food and sex included—I still have trouble with this when it comes to Bach.

Celibacy, because of the difficulties inherent in embracing it—let me rephrase that. Celibacy, because of the difficulties inherent in accepting it, celibacy is clearly a powerful prophetic statement concerning the reality of heaven. In other words, in the here and now, God has given to some men and women the gift of being able to live alone, without the need of a partner. The celibate's singleness is a witness to the truth of God's revelation of the future resurrected state of heaven. Celibates witness to themselves but, more especially, to those who are married—pointing out that sexuality is not the ultimate good, the be-all-and-end-all of human existence. It's too bad that celibacy currently suffers from bad press. Its prophetic message is not being heard. Another reason for this "non-hearing" is that few realize that celibacy is a prophetic message. Mandatory celibacy for priests might possibly come to an end in the next fifty years. Theologically, there's nothing to prevent that from happening. I, for one, think that celibacy should be optional for priests. But whatever happens, there will always be Catholics who will choose to be celibate "for the sake of the gospel." Notice how the prophetic dimension of celibacy fits into the notion that it is "for the sake of the gospel." It is "for the sake of the gospel" not because it gives a person more time and freedom to promulgate the "good news," but because it witnesses to the "good news" of the future state of resurrection.

The word for monk comes from the Greek word *monos,* meaning "alone." It is somewhat paradoxical that celibacy, i.e., aloneness, is a prophetic witness to heaven. Heaven, after all, is essentially union with God, not singleness. Wouldn't marriage be a better metaphor for heaven? An argument certainly can be made for marriage. Ephesians 5 points out that marriage is a figure for the indissoluble bond of love that exists between Jesus and the Church. The author quotes from Genesis: "'For this reason a man shall leave his father and mother, / and shall cling to his wife, / and the two shall be made into one.'" and then concludes, "This is a great foreshadowing; I mean that it refers to Christ and the church." This is, in fact, the theological underpinning of the Church's insistence that the bond of sacramental marriage is indissoluble—it is indissoluble because Christ's love for us is indissoluble. Both marriage and celibacy are figures, but only celibacy is prophetic in that it points to the future, not to the present. It's also prophetic in that, naturally speaking, it's impossible—it has no natural explanation. Its aura of the miraculous makes it a powerful witness to the future reality of the resurrected state of heaven. Of course, some of the same can be said of the steadfast love between a husband and wife; this too is altogether miraculous.

21

Bringing His Work to Completion Is My Food

*Doing the will of him who sent me
and bringing his work to completion
is my food. (Jn 4:34)*

*My Father is at work until now
and I am at work as well. . . .
The Son cannot do anything
    by himself—
he can do only what he sees the Father
doing. (Jn 5:17–20)*

*The Father loves me for this
that I lay down my life. . . . (Jn 10:17)*

*Whoever looks on me
is seeing him who sent me. (Jn 12:45)*

*Whoever has seen me has seen the
    Father . . .
it is the Father who lives in me
accomplishing his works. (Jn 14:9–10)*

This brings us to the greatest of all the biblical analogies: Jesus, icon of the Father. *Eikon* in Greek simply means image. Genesis reveals that humankind is made in the image of God. But to say that humankind is made in the image of God is far different from saying that Jesus is the image of God. The former nuance is quite generic and could equally be said of the angels. It simply means that man is like God in that he has a spiritual side, that he possesses intellect and free will. To say that Jesus is an image of God means much more; it means that Jesus reveals God. It means that Jesus is *the* icon of God. It means that to the extent that we know Jesus, we come to know God. The

introduction to Hebrews begins: "In times past God spoke
. . . through the prophets: in this, the final age, he has spoken to us through his Son. . . . This Son is the reflection of
the Father's glory, the exact representation of the Father's
being. . . ." It's true to say that if Jesus had not come onto
the human stage, we wouldn't know who God is. The pro-
logue to John's Gospel says: "No one has ever seen God. It
is God the only Son, ever at the Father's side, who has
revealed him" (Jn 1:18). Simply speaking, even with Jesus,
we still don't know God—and won't know him until we
are given the beatific vision and see him face to face. Perhaps it's more accurate to say that without Jesus we'd
know a whole lot less about who God is not. Terry Fullam,
the famous preacher, once related that in reading Colos-
sians 1 to his daughter ("He is the image of the Invisible
God") she blurted out: "I get it, Daddy. Jesus is God with
skin." Not bad at all!

The quotations from John at the beginning of this chapter will be of great help to us in deepening our idea of Jesus
as image of God. "Doing the will of him who sent me and
bringing his work to completion is my food." This one sentence contains a wealth of revelation. Jesus is, of course,
speaking here about the work of dying on the cross, but it's
curious that he refers to this work as "his work.", i.e., the
Father's work. Isn't Jesus' death on the cross Jesus' work?
Why does he call it the Father's work? If your twelve-year-
old takes out the garbage, then it's not your work but his
work—he gets the credit for it, not you. The answer to this
lies in Jesus' reference to the Father's will. Normally, when
one speaks of doing the will of God, one is referring to obedience to God's external will. Here Jesus is using the word
"will" in a totally different way. "Doing the will of him
who sent me" is indicative of Jesus' action, i.e., his suffering and death, being congruent not with the external will of
God but with the internal will of God. In other words, God
loves us so much that he would do anything to save us. He
would suffer for us, give his life for us, if needs be, but
being God, he cannot. Jesus, being God's Son, the image of
the invisible God, and human, is able and willing to do all
this for our sakes. This is why Jesus can say that "the Father

loves me for this that I lay down my life"—not because of his obedience but because he's a true son, a "chip off the old block." The Father loves Jesus in this context precisely because he externalizes his heart and mind, the invisible heart and mind of God.

The above interpretation is not to deny that obedience played any part in the "work of the Father." Jesus, after all, was human and, as human, he was obligated to obey God. It's more a question of primary and secondary motivations. Notice how the above interpretation sheds light on other scriptural problems. John 3:16, that famous verse one sees held up on banners while watching football on television, is at the heart of the gospel, but closer examination raises serious questions. "God so loved the world that he gave his only Son." Many parents have serious problems with this verse. What kind of father is God if he's willing to give his Son up to a horrible execution for the sake of others? I had a friend, Gloria, who was greatly upset with the notion that God would hand over his Son to death. She assured me that no parent would allow this. The above interpretation avoids that seeming parental cruelty and insensitivity on the part of the Father. Jesus, as Son, mirrors what's in the heart and mind of God—a heart and mind filled with unbelievable love and compassion for his children. Jesus generously gives his life for us because he is God's image; he gladly does for us what God would but cannot do.

A word about the Sacred Heart of Jesus is appropriate here. The real object of this devotion is not primarily the human heart of Jesus but the divine heart of God. It is the human heart of Jesus and the loving actions which proceed from that heart which reveal the divine heart of God.

Isaiah 49: 14 helps to shed light on this image: "But Zion said, 'The LORD has forsaken me; / my Lord has forgotten me. Can a mother forget her infant, / be without tenderness for the child of her womb? / Even should she forget, / I will never forget you. / See, upon the palms of my hands I have written your name." The figure here is somewhat unfamiliar. I've only experienced it once. Several years ago I met a royal Canadian mounted policeman while preaching at a parish in Nova Scotia. He had two unusual traits.

The first was that he didn't have a horse, and the second was that he had M O M tattooed on the middle fingers of his left hand and D A D tattooed on the middle fingers of his right hand. With those tattoos his parents were always before his eyes just as Zion, written on the Lord's palms, was always before his eyes. It can be argued that the prophetic words of Isaiah were finally fulfilled in the nail prints in the hands of the crucified Jesus. Our names are in the nail prints in Jesus' hands; they make visible the compassion and love that God has for his children.

This idea of identity between the work of God and the work of Jesus is also beautifully and tenderly depicted in a painting by Masaccio in the Church of Santa Maria Novella in Florence. (See the photo at the beginning of this chapter.) In the painting God the Father is standing behind the cross and holding up the arms of the crucified Jesus. I saw the same idea expressed in a stone sculpture in the church within the walls of Carcasonne, the church in which St. Dominic preached a lenten series. (See the photo at the beginning of Chapter 12, page 59.) Both works of art beautifully convey the idea that the work of Jesus is also, and more importantly, the work of the Father.

This idea of identification between the work of Jesus and the work of God is extremely valuable in getting rid of distorted notions about God. Some of the distortion comes from the Bible itself. We must always bear in mind that many parts of the Bible are very old and that God revealed himself progressively in time. Our knowledge of God, just as our knowledge in other disciplines, has evolved through the centuries. Since prophecy and revelation are necessarily transmitted through human thinking and understanding, their content is limited, filtered, and always somewhat distorted. It is to be expected that as time goes on, human thinking evolves positively and previous distortions attenuate. This is certainly true *vis-à-vis* our knowledge of God. The early books of the Bible portray a seemingly cruel and unloving God, a God who is warlike and vengeful, a God very much at odds with the God revealed by Jesus. I'm convinced that Jesus was killed primarily because he preached a God who was too loving and too compassionate for his hearers to bear. One of my annoyances is that many Christians read the Bible as they would the telephone directory, where the As are just as important as the Zs. In the Bible there is progressive revelation; the later books are more important than the earlier books. This means that the Old Testament must be interpreted by the New Testament. Identifying the work of Jesus with the work of the Father helps a great deal in removing distortions in our thinking about God.

Conclusion

In concluding, I want to congratulate you on your endurance and ask forgiveness if some of the reflections of God presented in these pages appear unseemly and irreverent. My purpose is certainly not to offend but rather to stimulate your own thinking and memory. God speaks to us and reveals himself most often in our ordinary but unique experiences. Your homework assignment now is to go through the photos you've been collecting over the years and find that picture of "Mr. Donut."